Case studies in Financial Management

M. G. Wright, B.Com., AACCA, FCIS

Senior Lecturer, School of Management,
The Polytechnic of Central London,
Consultant, Whitehead Consulting Group

McGRAW-HILL · LONDON

New York · Sydney · Toronto · Mexico · Johannesburg
Panama · Düsseldorf · Singapore

Published by
McGRAW-HILL Publishing Company Limited
MAIDENHEAD   BERKSHIRE   ENGLAND

---

07 094149 1

A/658, 150722

PRINTED AND BOUND IN GREAT BRITAIN
Photoset by BAS Printers Limited, Wallop, Hampshire

Case Studies in Financial Management

European business and management series

Consulting Editor
Dr W. F. Frank
Lanchester Polytechnic, Coventry

Other titles in the series:
Bourn: Studies in Accounting for Management Decision
Larkin: Work Study: Theory and Practice
Wallis: Accounting: A Modern Approach
Wright: Financial Management

Contents

Introduction   viii

Case

No. Name   1

✱1 ANYCOMPANY LIMITED
Analysis of company balance sheets and profit and
loss accounts for:
Profitability
Liquidity
Financial Ratios

2 LONGMEAD LIMITED   4
Forecasting the effect of extended trade credit on cash
needs and profitability

✱3 G. & B. MAXEY LIMITED   8
Investment in gravel deposits, equivalent to purchase
of stocks of material, investment appraisal

4 WARLANC LIMITED   10
Analysis of investment project

5 THE EXPANDING COMPANY LIMITED (A)   13
Appraising alternative investment projects

6 MACLIN PRODUCTS LIMITED   20
Uses and difficulties of application of breakeven
analysis

7 HINDOVER NOVELTIES LIMITED   25
Effect of fixed and variable cost recovery upon
reported profits

8 COMPUTER ANCILLARIES LIMITED   27
Pricing policy

9 CONVOLUTED TUBING LIMITED   38
   Determining sources of profitability and optimum
   product mix where there is a capacity constraint

10 THE EXPANDING COMPANY LIMITED (B)   43
   Evaluation of long-term contract against profitability
   requirements

11 CORFAIR INDUSTRIAL SERVICES LIMITED   45
   Analysis of sources and uses of funds

12 SUPERSHOPS LIMITED   49
   Forecasting cash needs and profitability requirements
   of a new business; methods of financing those needs

13 GRANGE SPORTSWEAR LIMITED   51
   The impact of expanding sales on bank credit

14 LEVY HARDWARE LIMITED   56
   Investment in expanding new company with an untried product; evaluation of business and terms

15 WENDOVER ELECTRONICS LIMITED   67
   Cash requirements for expanding manufacturing
   activities

16 BEDFORD INDUSTRIES LIMITED   72
   Cost of sources of funds

17 AMBLER ELECTRONICS LIMITED   77
   Setting the price for a new share issue

18 WILKINSON WARBURTON LIMITED   87
   Pricing a new issue on floatation

19 GW CONSTRUCTION COMPANY LIMITED   95
   Choosing between different sources of long-term funds

20 THOMPSONS (CONTRACTORS) LIMITED   104
   Estimating capital needs; financing choice; effect on
   return; analysis of risks

21 THE DE LA RUE COMPANY LIMITED (A)   111
   Financial Ratios; evaluation of company as an investment

22 THE DE LA RUE COMPANY LIMITED (B)   118
    Funds flow analysis and evaluation of the company

23 THE DE LA RUE COMPANY LIMITED (C1)   127
    Analysis of transactions and an investment in the
    company

24 THE DE LA RUE COMPANY LIMITED (C2)   140
    Study of reports and events for the company

25 UNIVERSE ELECTRONICS LIMITED   145
    Use of leasing as a financing alternative for capital
    investment

26 THE NULITE ELECTRICAL COMPANY   152
    LIMITED
    Corporate strategy—financial planning

27 PEARSON GROUP LIMITED   167
    Capital budgeting and the cost of capital

28 P. P. PAYNE & SONS LIMITED   173
    Take over bid—valuing bid terms

Introduction

This volume of cases is intended to be a companion volume to the author's *Financial Management* published by the McGraw-Hill Publishing Company Limited. The two volumes provide a comprehensive text and series of case studies for students and managers either on courses, such as the Diploma in Management Studies or Degree and Masters courses in which financial management forms an important element, or as part of individual firm's or industry's own training and education programmes for managers.

The cases are designed as far as possible to put the student in the actual decision situation. While, of course, this cannot be wholly possible because of the complexities of any actual business situation, the major points that the decision-maker would need to know are included. It does mean, however, that decisions will have to be taken, in some cases, with incomplete information or on the basis of students estimates of various factors based upon their own experience. This often proves troublesome to those unfamiliar with case studies, but a moment's thought will make one realize that in real life decisions are usually made on the same basis since information is often not available or there is not time to clear all the facts.

For the same reasons, it is rare for there to be a single right solution to the problems. What is required is a careful analysis of the available facts and the courses of action that are open to the decision-maker. These facts should be marshalled in such a way as to show the consequences of adopting each of the alternative courses of action available, both in quantifiable and non-quantifiable terms, and, finally, from this analysis, to make a choice as to the course of action that is most likely to provide the best results for the business within the context of its objectives.

This process will be greatly facilitated if the student puts himself in the shoes of the person who would be required to make the decision. He will then develop an awareness of the factors which are significant for the situation that he is concerned with and of which he must have a grasp, and will begin to learn to distinguish between the pertinent and the irrelevant in the case information.

Few business decisions are based upon applying a single technique to the problem. It should not be thought, therefore, that each case study relates to a single topic in *Financial Management*. The student must select those techniques which are applicable to the problem in hand. For example, a case dealing with the expansion of a business may require the use of breakeven analysis, cash flow forecasting, and DCF among others, as well as an analysis of the return and risks in the financing decision. For this reason, the cases are described by the type of problem that is involved rather than referred to different parts of the text in *Financial Management*.

In preparing this volume of cases, my sincere thanks are due to the Department of Education and Science and Cranfield Management School for permission to use the cases from the Management Case Research Unit; to Eric Ward for permission to use the Nulite Case; to John Simmonds for permission to use the Longmead case; and to the many institutions and companies both named and anonymous, who have given permission for other material to be used.

M. G. Wright

1

Anycompany Limited

Charles Agnew looked at the press announcement with unconcealed pleasure.

Anycompany Limited

The Board are happy to announce that Sales for the last year were the highest on record. Profits, although slightly down on last year, are still the second highest on record for the company. The preliminary figures are as follows:

	1968 £ 000s	1967 £ 000s
Sales	26 200	23 400
Profit before Interest and Taxation	2136	2341
Interest on Loan	390	390
Profit before Taxation	1746	1951
Corporation Tax at $42\frac{1}{2}\%$	694	770
Profit after Taxation	£1052	£1181

Final Dividend $12\frac{1}{2}\%$ ($12\frac{1}{2}\%$) making 20% (20%) for the year on the Ordinary Shares.

The day following this press announcement, Agnew left the United Kingdom for a short business trip to Turkey where he was concerned with a consultancy assignment with one of the major state enterprises. On his return to the UK, he saw in his accumulated post the published accounts for the year to 31 December 1968 for Anycompany Limited. Included were the group profit and loss account and balance sheet which are reproduced in Exhibits 1.1 and 1.2.

Seeing that these confirmed the preliminary press announcement, he looked gleefully to see what effect this continued high level of

1

activity had had upon the share price, since he held some 5000 shares in the company. To his surprise, he saw that the price had fallen to a new low of 12s 6d. He had not followed the price over the last year, and when he had last looked it up in the daily list in the *Financial Times* the share price had been 31s 6d.

He was aware that there had been a strong upward trend in the stock market up to the beginning of 1969 and could not reconcile this with the fall in the share price.

Meeting a friend of his, who was also in the consultancy field, but who dealt with financial management, he asked him his opinion of the company and what had happened over the last two or three years which had so jeopardized his investment. He still had available the previous year's accounts so was able to provide his friend with the three years' figures shown in Exhibits 1.1 and 1.2.

Exhibit 1.1 Anycompany Limited

Profit and Loss Account for the Years ended 31 December

	1966	1967	1968
	£ 000s	£ 000s	£ 000s
Sales	15 600	23 400	26 200
Operating Costs	13 899	20 533	23 469
Depreciation	157	526	595
Operating Profit before Interest	1544	2341	2136
Interest on Loan		390	390
Profit before Taxation	1544	1951	1746
Corporation Tax	624	770	694
Profit after Taxation	920	1181	1052
Less: Interest of Minority Shareholders	130	190	150
Profit Available to Shareholders	790	991	902
Dividends: (Gross)			
Preference	15	15	15
Ordinary (20%)	690	733	751
Retained Earnings	85	243	136
Share Price at 31 December	20s	30s	15s

Exhibit 1.2 Anycompany Limited
Balance Sheets as at 31 December

		1966 £ 000s		1967 £ 000s		1968 £ 000s
Fixed Assets (Net)						
Land and Buildings		920		1108		1340
Plant and Machinery		1465		5180		5665
Vehicles		45		62		115
		2430		6350		7120
Goodwill		3954		6540		6718
Trade Investments		920		210		750
Current Assets						
Stocks and WIP	4410		6350		7970	
Debtors and Prepayments	2611		3844		4980	
Marketable Securities	23		96		92	
Cash in Hand	40		75		5	
		7084		10 365		13 047
		14 388		23 465		27 635
Less: *Current Liabilities*						
Bank Overdraft	970		—		3500	
Creditors	2515		4660		4849	
Current Taxation	590		630		790	
Final Dividend	431		470		472	
		4506		5760		9611
Net Assets		9882		17 705		18 024
Shareholder's Funds						
7% Cumulative Preference Shares		250		250		250
Ordinary Shares of 5s each		3450		3760		3776
Share Premium		3644		3662		3670
Capital Reserve		1012		1120		1309
Retained Profit		612		855		991
		8968		9647		9996
6% Convertible Loan Stock 1990/95		—		6500		6500
Interest of Minority Shareholders in Subsidiary Companies		290		810		834
Future Taxation		624		748		694
		9882		17 705		18 024

2

Longmead Limited

Longmead Limited sells a package deal to the general public. The product, called All-in, was much in demand, and salesmen, employed on a commission basis by Longmead, sold the package direct to the public 'over the front door mat'.

The contents of All-in could be tailored to suit the individual customer, but basically it remained the same product. To meet the needs of their customers, Longmead divided the production processes of All-in into four stages. The package:
originated through the marketing department;
progressed to the design department;
from there to the assembly department;
then to the dispatch department.

The organization included a fifth department concerned only with general and administration affairs.

The current price of the All-in was £120. Terms had in the past been payment within 30 days net. No discounts were given. In the past, bad debts had been negligible.

The company had been in existence for some years. Profits before tax for the last five years were as follows:

	£
1968	55 100
1967	42 500
1966	41 280
1965	36 900
1964	31 060

The *after-tax* return on proprietors capital had averaged 6% to 7% over the years in question. The directors and shareholders of Longmead Limited considered this return to be far too low, and efforts had been made to see how this return could be improved.

In December 1969, the chief accountant of Longmead, Paul Brooks, was considering the company's cash budget for the first six months of the following year, i.e., January to June 1970. He had recently chaired the budget committee and was now about to draw up the company's master budget for the first half of 1970. Over the past few weeks, a number of meetings had been held with managers from all departments attending. The lead had been taken by the marketing department which had presented a strong case for offering deferred payments to would-be clients. By so doing, the department claimed sales would increase substantially. On the basis of offering clients six months in which to pay a sales forecast, based on market research, indicated that sales could double over the next six month period. On the basis of this forecast, all departments had drawn up preliminary budgets of cost and expenses in line with this level of activity. After discussion and some amendments by the budget committee, all the estimates were agreed. From these figures, shown in Exhibit 2.1, Paul Brooks was about to prepare the company's budget for the six months to 30 June 1970, a projected profit and loss account for that period and a projected balance sheet as at 30 June 1970.

The company's balance sheet as at the beginning of the six month period is shown in Exhibit 2.2.

Paul Brooks calculated that a stock of stationery to the value of £8200 would remain on hand at the end of June 1970 if the sales forecast was accurate.

All fixed costs are payable in the month for which they are incurred, and departmental variable costs *in the month following* that for which they were incurred. Other payments were to be made as indicated.

Cash from clients would be collectable on the basis of one-sixth of the sales price payable in the month of the sale and the remainder in equal instalments over the next five months.

Brooks was aware that trading in this way would lead to a temporary shortage of liquid funds. He thought that the cost of borrowing would be at the rate of 12% per annum, and that £11 600 of opening cash should be considered as cash float. The production process for All-in was quite short. There were no opening or closing stocks or work in progress at the beginning or end of any accounting period.

Exhibit 2.1 Longmead Limited

Budget Data for the First Six Months of 1970

Sales Forecast of All-in for the next six months of 1970 (Sales in units):

Jan.	*Feb.*	*March*	*April*	*May*	*June*	*Total*
3630	4290	5280	5940	6600	7260	33 000

Departmental Budgets for the six months were as follows:

Note: Departmental Managers were held responsible for the direct costs applicable to their department. Such costs were divided into:

Fixed: i.e., salaries, wages, rentals of special equipment, etc.
Variable: costs arising from the production of each package, i.e., basic components, specialized services, royalty fees, etc.

All costs and expenses which could not be specifically allocated to departments were not apportioned but charged as general company overheads to the profit and loss account. These latter costs were held to be the responsibility of the general manager.

1. *Marketing department*
   Direct costs.
   Fixed: £12 000.
   Variable: 10% of the final selling price of each package deal paid in month following the sale.

2. *Design department*
   Direct costs.
   Fixed (including depreciation of £6000): £36 000.
   Variable: £60 per package.

3. *Processing—assembly department*
   Direct costs.
   Fixed (including depreciation of £22 000): £108 000.
   Variable: £30 per package.

4. *Dispatch department*
   Direct costs.
   Fixed (including depreciation of £2000): £14 000.
   Variable: £5 per package.

5. *Administrative department*
   Direct costs.
   Fixed (including depreciation of £1000): £65 000.

6. *Other general costs and expenses*
   Rent, rates, heating, lighting, etc., for the entire premises. (*Note:* Paid in two equal instalments in March and June): £100 000.
   Delivery of stationery stocks. (*Note:* Payable February): £4000.
   Payment on account of custom built equipment to be delivered in August. Payment due in May: £95 000.

Exhibit 2.2 Longmead Limited

Balance Sheet as at 31 December 1969

	£			£
Fixed Assets		*Share Capital*		
At Cost	440 000	300 000 Ordinary Shares		
Less Depreciation		of £1 each issued and		
to date	136 000	Fully Paid		300 000
		Retained Earnings		215 000
	304 000			
				515 000
Current Assets				
Stock of		*Future Tax Liability*		22 000
Stationery	5400	*Current Liabilities*		
Debtors	336 000	Trade Creditors	183 000	
Cash	91 600	Tax Due 1 Jan.		
	433 000	1970	17 000	
				200 000
	£737 000			£737 000

3

G. and B. Maxey Limited

GRAVEL
Extensive Gravel-Bearing Land
FOR SALE
Beds   Price £110 000
Further Details—Write Box 185

Jim Darrall passed the above advertisement which he had cut from his weekend papers over to his codirector Bob Carter. 'That looks a promising lead,' he said, 'for the new deposits that we shall be needing in that area over the next few years. You recall that Traver's report pointed to the early ending of the workings at our Boxton plant and the need to provide alternative sources of supply within the next eighteen months. I know that cash is tight at the present time, but I think that we should follow up this prospect.'

'OK, Jim, I'll write in for details and if they seem suitable I'll go along and see the vendors,' Bob Carter replied, tucking the clip into his wallet.

Some two weeks later, the two directors held an informal meeting to discuss the details that Bob Carter had acquired from the vendors. He first of all outlined the discussions that he had had.

'The property consists of good quality gravel bearing land which should yield approximately 600 000 cubic yards of gravel. Taking into account the acess to the site and our own likely requirements, I think that this would last us approximately six years. The owners are asking £110 000, but I get the feeling from my discussions with them that they will settle for £100 000 in cash, or by an extended payments basis to the total of £120 000. A suggested basis for the

8

latter would be £20 000 down and quarterly payments of £10 000 each quarter until the total is paid. Simon tells me that the Boxton plant is pretty well clapped out and we would need to install new plant to work these deposits. John Collins has obtained some quotes, and he reckons that we would have to lay out about £80 000 to cover this, although this would be offset to some extent by the investment grants.'

'That sounds all right to me, Bob,' Jim Darrall replied, 'it certainly seems to fit in with our forecast requirements and is about the right size. What are our likely earnings if we worked it over the six year period? I think that we should get some idea of this before we go any further. Simon was pretty scathing at our last board meeting about the return that we earn on investments. We're thinking of recommending to the board that we undertake a programme to lift our after tax return on investments from 10% to $12\frac{1}{2}\%$. It would be interesting to see whether or not this investment would provide us with the needed return.'

'Well, Jim, we have worked out some data for you although this has not been worked up into a formal investment appraisal structure yet. As you know, we work on an average royalty for gravel of 4s per cubic yard. The profit estimated from the new workings is around £30 000 before charging any depreciation, but after charging the relevant royalty value. This would provide an adequate return on the £80 000 investment in plant that we would have to make.'

'I think that the problem is not quite so simple as that, Bob. Simon was talking recently about discounted cash flow. From what I understand of what he said, we would have to take more factors into account than that. I know that we will still have the land when the workings are finished, but whether or not this will be a liability or an asset I'm not sure. What if the government or local authorities begin to take more interest in land restoration? It might take £50 000 to do this.'

Questions
1. What alternatives face the company at the present time?
2. What factors do you think are relevant to this decision?
3. Would you proceed with the purchase and do you think you would require any further information?

4

Warlanc Limited

Following some years of difficult trading conditions in the middle and late 'sixties, the directors of Warlanc have been considering the formulation of a corporate strategy for the 'seventies and, possibly, the 'eighties. While the proposals for the entry of the United Kingdom into the European Economic Community are still unresolved, the paper-making industry, within which the company operates, is still subject to conditions of considerable uncertainty. Only when the relations between the UK and both the European Free Trade Area and the Common Market have been finally resolved and, in particular, the position of the Scandinavian producers is known, will some of the uncertainties be removed.

The target that the board has set for profitability over the planning period that it is considering is a return on capital employed after tax of 12%, and as a preliminary to the formal publication of its plan *Forward to the Seventies*, which is to be circulated to all managerial staff, the board has minuted that no investments will be made unless the return that the investment offers is in excess of that figure.

As a part of its plan for improving profits, the board has been considering a proposal to increase the company's coating capacity. This can be achieved by the conversion of a machine, currently making MF printings, through the addition of a coating station before the last section of dryers. This will enable the machine to produce machine coated art.

The capital cost of the coating station, and the ancillary equipment that would be required, is estimated at £100 000. The variable costs of operating the machine would be approximately 60% of the additional sales that it would produce and the fixed costs, including £10 000 per annum depreciation, would be £30 000 per annum.

The processes in the paper-making industry are peculiar, in that the paper-making 'machine' is really an integrated plant. It consists of a framework and sole plates to which are added the plant for each of the processing stages, e.g., pulper, flow box, couch roll, suction couch, press roll, etc. To these would be added machine drives, piping, pumps, and so on. The basic framework may well have a life of 40 to 50 years, but the various parts that are added will, of course, be replaced at much more frequent intervals.

At the time the board were considering the proposal for the conversion, the Government operated an investment incentive scheme which provided for the payment of a cash grant (investment grant) to firms in certain industries (which included the paper-making industry) which invest in new production plant and machinery. The requirement that the plant should be new has provided some confusion in the industry, since, in terms of new paper-making machines, most of the new investment would not qualify for the grant.

A circular from the Board of Trade (which operated the grant scheme at that time) set out proposals for remedying this situation. That circular stated:

As paper-making is a 'continuous flow' process it is considered necessary, in order that the paper-making industry should not be treated less favourably than other industries using more conventional machines or equipment, to allow certain parts of a paper-making machine to be accorded 'entity' treatment (see paragraph 4 below) when deciding whether to accept the cost of replacing them as approved capital expenditure. It must be emphasized that special considerations have been applied and the Board would not necessarily be prepared to accord the same treatment to any similar items used in processes other than paper-making.

. . . In all other cases the straight replacement of a part of a machine by a part of the same design is not eligible for grant. If, however, a part which is not accepted as an entity is replaced by a new part which effects an improvement in the performance or range of the machine, the grant will be payable on the improvement element (that is the difference between the cost of providing a straight replacement and that of providing the improved part) provided that this element is £25 or more . . .

The company's mill is in the south of Lancashire and will not therefore qualify for any grant at the higher development area rate.

On past experience, it is believed that the Inland Revenue will allow a writing-down allowance at the rate of 20% straight line.

The addition is expected to have an economic life of about ten years, after which the future of the paper-making machine as a whole would be reviewed. The coating station would have no value at the end of the period.

Forecast of Sales

The marketing manager has prepared for consideration by the Board an estimate of the additional sales that would be won. The figures are as follows:

	£		£
1971	50 000	1972	100 000
1973	120 000	1974	150 000
1975	150 000	1976	150 000
1977	150 000	1978	120 000
1979	90 000	1980	80 000

It is expected that increases in stores, work in progress, and those in respect of debtors and creditors, are expected to increase working capital by some 30% of the sales value.

After consideration of the outline of the project, the board asked for a full appraisal to be carried out of the rate of profitability that the investment would offer so that it could be compared with the profitability criteria that they have laid down. Further, they have asked that consideration should be given to the situation should sales not reach the forecast levels and, consequently, profits are £3000 per year lower than forecast. They are not altogether happy about the estimated ten year life of the coating station, and have asked for the appraisal to be carried out, in addition, on the basis of an eight year life only.

5

The Expanding Company Limited (A)

The Expanding Company Limited has been established as a medium-sized civil engineering and building company for a number of years. Based upon a prewar family company, it has deliberately restricted its field of operations to the London region and the South-West. Its late managing director was concerned to see that the management of the company could adequately supervise the sites that were being worked upon currently. While he and his fellow directors were resident in the area of operations, this policy paid off, with a small management team closely controlling each site.

The founding director died suddenly as a result of a car accident in May 1966, and for nearly twelve months the financial affairs of the business were dominated by the need to provide for the payment of death duties. His death also exposed the fundamental weakness of the management team: as a dominant element in the business, his personality held together a team whose members were mediocre when considered as individuals.

The death duty problem was finally resolved by the executors selling the whole of the late managing director's shares (comprising nearly 60% of the total ordinary shares) to a merchant bank: Feldmans (Industrial Bankers) Limited. Approximately 10% of the remaining shares were held by the other directors and the remainder by the public, the company being quoted on the Provincial Stock Exchange.

Feldmans were interested in a number of industrial companies. They obtained interests in them in similar circumstances to the acquisition of the interest in ECL; they also provided finance for expanding companies together with the acquisition of a share in the equity.

In the board discussions which preceded the purchase of the ECL shares, the declared policy for that acquisition was to improve the level of profitability to the target rate set for the parent company, and then to dispose of the shares that were held in excess of 51%.

The first priority in the development of ECL was seen to be the need to strengthen the management team; this was to be centred upon a high level replacement for the late managing director. After a great deal of searching and pursuing of contacts in the industry, Mr F. C. Willis was appointed as managing director. Mr Willis has had a wide range of experience on both the civil engineering and building sides of the industry. For the last four years, he had been employed as a regional director of overseas operations for an international group with an American parent. Prior to this he had held appointments as contracts manager and site manager for one of the major UK companies.

The board of directors of Feldmans considered the second priority in the development of ECL was to expand its area of activities and so provide a much wider base of operations based upon the strengthened management team. The bank has access to adequate funds for investment provided that the return is right. Its industrial investments are very diverse and new opportunities are continually arising for investment. Usually, such opportunities offer a return on investment in excess of 12% after tax, and there is a board minute to the effect that no investments will be made which return less than 10% after tax. It maintains at its head office a small team of specialists to whom all major investment proposals are submitted for appraisal and report to the parent company board. It is currently considering a number of investment proposals with returns in the range 12–20% after tax.

In the six months since his appointment, Mr Willis has strengthened the management of the business with a number of key appointments, and has been discussing with colleagues possible strategies for the development of the business. Initially, these discussions have been on the relative merits of expansion on a geographical basis versus those of a broadening of the type of work that the company undertakes. Senior managers, as well as the directors, were alerted to report openings which they came across.

At one of his weekly meetings with the managing director of Feldmans, Maurice Feldman, Willis was informed of a recent meeting that Feldman had had with one of his continental associates.

This associate has close financial links with a major continental construction company, DC ag. DC had recently developed and marketed a new design for prefabrication of factory units off site and of assembly and provision of services on site. Having established this technique in its home territory, it was now looking for suitable licensing opportunities overseas. Feldman ascertained that DC would be prepared to consider licensing ECL to use its processes and designs on the basis of a lump sum payment and royalty, the terms of which would have to be negotiated. Willis was instructed to visit the offices of DC and given the authority to negotiate licensing terms within specific limits laid down by the board.

The meetings that followed lasted two weeks, and during them Willis was most impressed by the system that was used by DC. Before returning to the UK, heads of agreement were drawn up for the terms of the licence for consideration by the two boards. Apart from the provisions for the exchange of technical information, the important clauses were those concerned with the payments to be made by ECL. These were finalized after much haggling as a down payment of £120 000 and an annual royalty on sales of $2\frac{1}{2}\%$. Should the level of annual royalties fall below £20 000 a minimum figure of £20 000 was to apply. The sales value on which the royalty applies comprises the full value of the units including charges for design and services.

These proposals were considered at a joint meeting of the boards of Feldmans and ECL. It was felt that the high cost of the licence arrangements would mean that the area of activities would require a wide geographical spread to achieve the volume of sales that would make it a paying proposition. Before making a final decision on the matter, the board of Feldmans called for full data on:

1. Alternative geographical areas for expansion.

2. Assessment of demand in each area.

3. Forecast cost levels and proposed selling prices.

4. The implications that the proposals would have for the traditional civil engineering and building division.

5. Forecast of capital requirements.

6. An assessment of breakeven volume.

The report of the board of ECL to its parent contains, among other factors, the following information:

Location

Two geographical areas of expansion were examined. The prosperous and rapidly growing Midlands conurbation, together with the South Lancashire and South Yorkshire areas, was thought to make a manageable region in view of the recent improvements in the lines of communication in the region. Not only would it offer a higher level of potential demand for the proposed units, but control, both within the region and from head office, could be more easily exercised.

On the other hand, there were considerable attractions in operating in a development area. The inducements to set up business in these areas which are provided by the Government would reduce considerably the capital requirements of the expansion. If this alternative was chosen, the region would be based upon Newcastle-upon-Tyne to cover the Tyneside and Wearside areas, with possible outlying activities in the industrial belt between Glasgow and Edinburgh. The advantages of government grants would be offset, to some extent, by a smaller potential demand and higher management costs for the region.

Forecast Demand

After a study of likely trends in each region examined, the level of potential and effective demand were estimated as follows:

	Midlands	North-east and Scotland
Potential demand for units	1200 in 1969 rising to 1400 in 1972	1000 in 1969 rising to 1100 in 1972
Proportion of business that the company could capture	$22\frac{1}{2}\%$	25%

Selling Price

The proposed units would sell at £7500 each, and to this would be added approximately £1500 to cover design and services.

Effect of Civil Engineering Business

It was felt that the representation that would be required to launch and maintain the new units could be utilized to promote an extension of the civil engineering activities. The promotional activities that would be needed to make the company and its products known, could easily be adapted to include the civil engineering side, and the fact that the company would have a broader base of activities in the region would aid the sale of units.

The likely levels of civil engineering sales that would be achieved in the two regions are, in the Midlands, £1·6 million per year; in North-East and Scotland, £1·2 million per year.

Taking together all types of activity in the new regions, it was expected that it would take about four years from establishing the regional office to build up its maximum potential. This build-up would be achieved in approximately equal steps each year.

Cost of Establishing the Regional Office

1. *Premises*: to purchase £260 000 per year
   to rent   £28 000 per year

2. *Regional office costs* (based upon an output of 250 units per year)
   Salaries: £78 000 p.a.
   Travelling: £18 000 p.a.
   Other Expenses (other than depreciation):   £69 000 p.a.
   Present HO costs which would be allocated to the
      regional office   £45 000 p.a.

3. *Overheads of manufacturing unit* (based upon an output of 250 units per year): £117 000 p.a.
   It is estimated that the costs of operating the regional office in the Midlands would be approximately £50 000 less than the above figures.

4. *Costs of prefabricated units*
   Production and installation costs of units: £6200 each
   Design and Services   £1200 per unit
   The variable part of the manufacturing overhead would amount to approximately £200 per unit manufactured.

5. *Civil engineering costs*
   The company aims to earn a margin of $12\frac{1}{2}\%$ on contracts before charging depreciation and head office and regional office expenses.

6. *Life of plant*
   It is estimated that the plant would have a life of ten years. At the end of that time, changes in the technology of the industry and market demand changes would probably require new methods to be introduced. The value of the plant at the end of this period is estimated as:

17

Plant and Machinery—Factory:		£8500
	Erection and services:	£11 000
	Civil engineering:	£31 000

7. *Investment*

Plant and machinery for prefabrication of units	£270 000
Equipment for erecting units and providing services	£320 000
Additional equipment for civil engineering activities	£224 000

Replacement of worn out equipment at the end of year 5 in the programme would cost £25 000.

Questions:
1. Analyse the proposals and comment.
2. What recommendations would you make to the board of Feldmans?

Exhibit 5.1 The Expanding Company Limited (A)

Balance Sheet as at 31 December 1967

USES OF FUNDS (£ 000s)

Fixed Assets	Cost	Depreciation	Net
Freehold Land and Buildings	210	—	210
Leasehold Land and Buildings	120	45	75
Plant and Equipment	963	346	617
Mobile Equipment and Vehicles	76	42	34
	1369	433	936

Goodwill		447
Current Assets		
Value of Work in Hand for Clients	3695	
Less Payments Received on Account	2864	
	831	
Debtors	676	
Cash in Hand and at Bank	112	
		1619
		3002
Current Liabilities		
Owing to Creditors and Subcontractors	1085	
Tax Payable 1 Jan. 1968	134	
Dividend	100	
		1319
Total Net Assets		£1683

The Expanding Company Limited (A)

SOURCES OF FUNDS
Share Capital

Authorized 4 000 000 Ordinary Shares of 5s each	1000
Issued 3 000 000 Ordinary Shares of 5s each	750
Share Premium	110
Capital Reserves	194
Retained Profits	249
	1303
7% Debenture 1985/87	300
Tax Payable 1 Jan. 1969	80
	£1683

Exhibit 5.2 The Expanding Company Limited

Profit and Loss Account for the Year to 31 December 1967

	(£ 000s)
Sales	6359
Direct Costs of Contracts and Site Overheads	5712
Profit on Contracts	647
Company Overheads	428
Operating Profit	219
Debenture Interest	21
Net Profit	198
Tax	80
Profits after Tax	118
Dividend	100
Profit for Year Retained	18
Brought forward from Previous Years	231
Carried forward	£249

A/658.15 D722 **19**

6

Maclin Products Limited

Howard Maclin, managing director of Maclin Products Limited, is currently considering proposals for operations for the following year, preparatory to holding discussions with the management committee at their meeting to be held later in the week. Maclin Products is an old established company which manufactures three basic types of electronic equipment under its own brandname; it has enjoyed a steady pattern of growth over the last five years.

The estimated results for the year 19X1, based upon nine months actual figures and three months estimated figures, are shown in Exhibit 6.1, and are to form the basis of the budgets for the following year adjusted for an expected growth rate of 20–50%. This expected growth rate was decided upon at a preliminary budget meeting held the previous week. The forthcoming committee meeting is to enable the functional executives to report back on the implications of the planned growth rate for their departments, and to assess the likely implications for profits.

Howard Maclin recently attended a senior management seminar at which the speaker discussed the use of breakeven analysis to show the likely effect of changes in volume upon profits, and he thought that the technique would be useful to show basic trends in a business in a situation such as that in which his own firm found itself at the present time. Between the two meetings, he decided to try to use it to explore the effect of the change in volume that was being forecast so that it could be used as the basis for discussion at the meeting. Ben Whitaker, his accountant, was requested to analyse the activities for the current year in terms of fixed and variable costs and to use the results as the basis of a breakeven chart showing forecast profits.

The breakeven chart prepared by Whitaker is shown in Exhibit

6.2. In his report that accompanied the chart, Whitaker set out the basis of his division of costs between fixed and variable. The items included in the profit and loss account figures marked with an asterisk in Exhibit 6.1 were treated as fixed costs, the remainder as variable. His report then proceeded,

Using as a basis for your next year's sales the lowest estimate of the sales increase, i.e., 20%, would bring the profit up from £65 000 to £135 000 or double the 19X1 figure. If you manage to hit the 50% sales increase, then the profit would soar to approximately £227 000. This would provide the funds to put a great deal more pressure behind our selling effort.

Feeling somewhat enthused by this glimpse of the possibilities for his business, Howard Maclin decided to take Whitaker with him to the meeting so that he could present the breakeven chart as an overall picture of what the operating budget should show for the following year.

Shortly after lunch the following Friday, Whitaker presented copies of his data to the members of the management committee. Besides Howard Maclin and himself, there were present Andrew Loughlin, the production manager; Dennis Potter, the personnel manager; Bernard Devlin, sales manager; and Brendan Coney, the head of research.

Bernard Devlin set the ball rolling by criticising the projection of sales. 'I can quite see,' he said, 'why the range of sales expansion is within the capacity of the firm. What we must bear in mind, however, is that our product B has passed its peak performance and is likely to decline by some 20% in volume over the next two years. After all, product C was introduced specifically to provide a low price alternative to B in some uses where the specifications are less critical, as well as to exploit hitherto untapped demand. Product A is still in the stage of gaining market acceptance. I would guess that A and C between them will replace any lost turnover from B and, in addition, provide you with the required sales volume increase.'

'Hold on a minute, Barney,' interjected Andrew Loughlin, 'product C is a very competitive product planned to be produced in quantity on sophisticated and expensive machines with a small labour content. As I figure it, if sales of B drop back 10% to around £540 000, then A and C between them will have to turn in extra sales of £320 000, or, if the overall 50% increase is achieved, £710 000. We just have not got the plant to push out that sort of volume. The latter figure postulates doubling our capacity for C, and means taking up the spare capacity and adding a few more machines. Seeing that our plant for making C cost £150 000 when we bought it some two years ago, I reckon that we should need a similar investment now. With A, we could probably get the output by spending some £30 000. Whichever way you figure it we are going to need more space.'

'But look, Andy,' remarked Devlin 'we put C on the market as a low-cost product to meet the competition. We are screwed right down by the market, as far as price is concerned. Our only way to make this really profitable, and, as I recall, this was the basis on which we agreed to its introduction two years or so ago, is through volume. We are getting volume through now and it is up to you boys to back us up with the goods.'

At this point, Brendan Coney finished lighting his pipe and said, 'From the research point of view, I don't think the pressures are going to come off product B. I hear that Jerry Lyndon's firm may be coming up with an alternative device which will make some inroads into our market. I think that your sales projections for B may be a bit optimistic.'

Dennis Potter had remained silent up to this point, but he broke in now by saying, 'Well, I think you both ought to get your views clear on this point. Although our new plant is highly automated, any new staff that we would need should be high quality, and we ought to give them some training on the job. These machines are too expensive to entrust to unskilled labour. The level of expansion that you are talking about will put quite a strain on our recruiting and training staff. It also occurs to me that the cloakrooms and other services for staff will be overcrowded, and we may have to bring forward our plans to put up our £30 000 new office block to release accommodation for this. What sort of extra supervision are you going to need?'

After considerable argument along the same lines Howard Maclin held up his hands and said, 'Just a moment, you fellows. We're only looking at a tentative projection of volume. What you, Barney, are saying about our intentions for product C when we introduced it, rings a bell with me. But perhaps now is the time to review our policy. Certainly, the margins thrown up in the figures Ben has shown us indicate that this may not be the money-spinner that we thought. Before we hare off and spend a lot of money on plant and take on new staff, we ought to look at some of the implications of what we have been talking about for our long-term profitability. I'm quite sure that Ben will have to go back to the drawing board and look at his figures and breakeven chart again. There is more to this breakeven business than I thought.'

Exhibit 6.1 Maclin Products Limited
Actual and Estimated Profit and Loss Account 19X1

	Actual (1.1.19X1 to 30.9.19X1)	*Estimated* (1.10.19X1 to 31.12.19X1)	*Total*
	£ 000s	£ 000s	£ 000s
Sales	964	336	1300
Cost of Goods Sold			
Materials	242	83	325
Labour	335	115	450
Factory Supervision	36	13	49*
Other Factory Indirect Labour	88	32	120
Consumables	30	12	42
Power and Light	14	6	20
Rent and Rates	27	8	35*
Depreciation	90	30	120*
Total	862	299	1161
Gross Profit	102	37	139
Selling Expenses			
Salaries	24	8	32*
Commission	13	5	18
General Company Expenses	18	6	24*
Net Profit Before Tax	47	18	65

Exhibit 6.2 Maclin Products Limited: Breakeven Chart

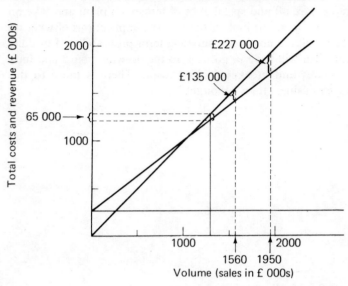

Volume (sales in £ 000s)

Exhibit 6.3 Maclin Products Limited
Cost Build-up of Products

Product	A	B	C
	£	£	£
Sales Price	5·0	6·0	4·0
Costs: Variable	4·5	3·8175	3·11
Fixed	0·4	1·905	0·5
Profit per Unit	0·1	0·2775	0·39
Number of Units Sold			
(Actual and Estimated 19X1)	80 000	100 000	75 000
Machine Hours per Unit	0·5	0·4	1·5

7

Hindover Novelties Limited

Mr J. Hinds was preparing to present to the forthcoming meeting of the board a report on the activities of the firm for the month of June. His assistant, Jim Bolsover, who is the son of the Chairman, has recently analysed the activities of the business in the form of a break-even graph (see Exhibit 7.1). This showed that in May, when sales were 15 000 units, profits should have been in the order of £7500 and, apart from minor variances, this rate of profit had been reported in the profit and loss account.

For June, the volume of sales had been 17 500 units, and, on this basis, he had been expecting a substantial improvement in the profit rate. He was therefore considerably shocked when Frank Jones, his accountant, reported to him that the balance on the profit and loss account for the month was less than that for the previous month (see Exhibit 7.2).

The company operated a standard costing system which provided for flexible expense budgets. Designed to provide a more meaningful control over the managers concerned, the level of budgeted overheads were adjusted by the variable element to the actual level of activity achieved. The normal volume of sales on which the budgeted overhead recovery was based was 20 000 units per month.

Questions
1. What is the breakeven volume for the company?
2. At the volume of sales indicated on the breakeven chart for May, what would have been the exact amount of profit?
3. How many units were produced in June?
4. What level of profit would Mr Hinds have been expecting in June, and what were the reasons for the difference?

Exhibit 7.1 Hindover Novelties Limited: Breakeven Chart

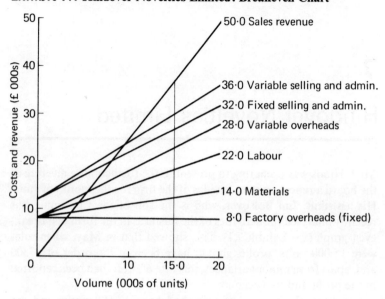

50·0 Sales revenue
36·0 Variable selling and admin.
32·0 Fixed selling and admin.
28·0 Variable overheads
22·0 Labour
14·0 Materials
8·0 Factory overheads (fixed)

Exhibit 7.2 Hindover Novelties Limited
Profit and Loss Account for June

			£
Sales (17 500 Units)			43,000
Standard Cost of Sales			24 500
			18 500
Materials:	Price Variance	(640)	
	Usage Variance	200	
			(440)
Labour:	Rate Variance	200	
	Time Variance	–	
			200
Overheads:	Expense	300	
	Volume	(4000)	
	Efficiency	–	
			(3700)
Manufacturing Profit			14 560
Selling and Administrative Expenses			8100
Net Profit			£6460

8

Computer Ancillaries Limited*

Mr J. Ainsworth was planning to start marketing magnetic tapes for use on computers in October 1965. Although much of the groundwork had been done already, no final decision had been taken on the scale of the initial operation, or on the pricing, or on the marketing plan, when Mr Ainsworth was interviewed by the casewriter in August 1965. A new company was being formed to undertake the marketing of ancillary equipment associated with computer installations, but at that time neither Mr Ainsworth nor the company had been given a title. This company, to be named Computer Ancillaries Limited (CA) hereafter, was to be formed as a subsidiary of Engdata Limited and had an initial capital of £7500; Mr Ainsworth was to be appointed the general manager.

Engdata Limited

In early 1963, a company, by the name of Advanced Engineering Services (AES), had been established with the object of providing a wide range of services to users of electronic computers. The activities planned for the company at that time included a consultancy service, a company to provide computational services to the engineering industry, and a marketing organization for ancillary equipment associated with computer installations. In July 1964, Dugdale Enterprises Limited, a company with a variety of interests, joined with AES in forming a holding group, Engdata Limited, which was to comprise three subsidiary companies; these were Engdata Consul-

*Case material of the Management Case Research Unit, Cranfield, Bedford, England, and prepared as a basis for class discussion. This case was made possible through the cooperation of a British company which remains anonymous. Cases are not designed to illustrate correct or incorrect handling of business situations. Reproduced by kind permission of the Cranfield School of Management.

tants, a computational services company due to start operations in the summer of 1965, and the marketing company (CA). The injection of new capital from Dugdale Enterprises enabled funds to be made available for the purchase of an ICT 1904 computer. The directors of Engdata considered that a large market existed for an organization of a type which could make computational services available to small engineering firms for whom the purchase of their own computer installation, at a cost of £200 000–£300 000, would not be economical.

Although the formation of a marketing company had been part of the original AES concept, firm plans for its establishment were not made until the summer of 1965. Ainsworth, who was selected as the general manager designate, was an economics graduate from the London School of Economics, and had been employed by a large electronic manufacturing company prior to joining AES as a consultant.

In July 1965, Engdata moved into a recently completed modern office block in Slough. This building would eventually house all three companies, including the ICT 1904 computer installation. The marketing company was allocated an area of 250 square feet for office accommodation and storage.

The Marketing Company

A company considering the purchase of a computer would invariably carry out a detailed analysis of different makes and models of computer, and their associated software, before a final selection was made. However, in this case, little attention was paid to the choice of the many items of ancillary equipment used in conjunction with a computer installation, much of which was not designed for that particular application. The term 'ancillary' covers a wide range of equipment and includes such items as furniture, card trays, magnetic and paper tapes, spools, splicers, and even tape library systems.

It was thought that a company specializing in the marketing of ancillary equipment designed to meet the needs of computer installations would be assured of success and that Engdata was favourably placed to fill this need. Although it was intended, initially, to market only one product, magnetic tapes, the aim of CA was gradually to extend the range of equipment until the company was able to satisfy a comprehensive list of its customers' requirements. CA was to remain solely a factoring organization, but it was the company's intention to have equipment manufactured to its own specifications at a later date. In 1965, there was no furniture designed specifically for use with computers. It was considered that there was a need for a range of chairs, desks, and tables, to be designed ergonomically in relation to the displays and controls of the computer systems with which they would be used. Another idea was to devise a library system for magnetic tapes using documentation designed and sold by CA. The association of Engdata with Dugdale Enterprises could be of great assistance in these plans, for within the Dugdale group there was a furniture manufacturer, a firm producing small plastic and aluminium components, several small general engineering companies, and an office equipment company. These companies would be able to manufacture a variety of articles to CA's specifications. CA's close contact with computer users and the experience of the other Engdata companies would ensure that design specifications were well suited to their customers' requirements.

However, as the company had a capitalization of only £7500 and an operating budget of £11 700 for the first year's operations, Mr Ainsworth realized that he must initially confine himself to marketing a product which was already available: the cost of the design and manufacture of entirely new products would be high in relation to the funds available and must wait until it could be financed from earnings. He estimated that for a quite simple design in plastic the cost of dies and tools alone for an injection moulding would be as high as £3000. It was for this reason that it was decided that CA would begin by marketing only one product, a new high quality ½ in. magnetic tape manufactured by a large British company.

Magnetic Tape Market

The marketing of a new brand of magnetic tape was thought to offer extremely good prospects of early success for a number of reasons. The total number of computer installations in the United Kingdom had risen from 138 in 1960 to 1133 in 1965 (see Exhibits 8.1 and 8.2), and it was estimated that there would be a further fivefold expansion in the years 1965–70. The increase in the use of magnetic tape, however, would be even greater than these figures indicated, since the proportion of new computers using magnetic rather than paper tapes was rising rapidly. In addition, it could be expected that existing computers would be applied to new data processing functions, with a consequent increase in the number of tapes in use. There would also be a rising demand for replacement tapes. The life of a magnetic tape varied with the amount it was used, but, on average, it was estimated to be about one year.

Magnetic tapes fell into four classes: video, audio, analogue, and digital, the last two being the types used in computers. There were a number of British companies producing magnetic tapes, but, so far, they had concentrated on the lower quality audio tapes catering mainly for the sound-recording mass market. Mr Ainsworth estimated that 80% of the tapes used by digital computers in the UK were supplied by the Minnesota Mining and Manufacturing Company (3Ms) who imported them from the United States. Another American Company, Memorex, which claimed approximately 20% of the market for tapes in the USA, had been selling tapes in the UK for about a year, with some success. Computape, another American company, had recently appointed UK agents. Mr Ainsworth knew of no British company, other than his own supplier, which was contemplating the manufacture of magnetic tapes suitable for digital applications. This situation could well change, however, as the market for digital quality tapes expanded, particularly since it was relatively easy for a manufacturer of audio tapes to produce digital tapes, for both could be made on essentially the same equipment.

In spite of the recent moves by Memorex and Computape, the UK market still remained a near monopoly for 3Ms. This established position was strengthened by 3Ms' sales to the computer manufacturers; both ICT and IBM, for example, used 3Ms' magnetic tape. Thus, it was natural for a computer-user to reorder from 3Ms when he needed an additional supply of magnetic tape, since this was the make which had been supplied with the computer when new. 3Ms, therefore, held its position in the market for replacement tapes to a great extent through its sales to the computer manufacturers. Mr Ainsworth realized that, if CA were to succeed in breaking into this market, he must persuade users to change their habit of automatically reordering the same tapes. This he felt confident could be done, provided he could convince the buyers of the technical and economic merits of the tapes CA would market. This would not be unduly difficult for the buyers were technical men who would be prepared to assess the new tape on its technical merit; they would also appreciate any cost-saving through lower prices since they were usually under pressure from their company to reduce expenditure. In short, the present market could be described as one in which magnetic tapes were bought rather than sold. It was this situation which CA intended to change.

Preliminary Marketing Plans

While there was no evidence of widespread dissatisfaction among users of 3Ms' tape, Ainsworth believed that this was due to complacency resulting from the lack of alternatives from which to choose. Nevertheless, discussions with computer-users had given him reason to believe that the users were not entirely pleased with the service they were receiving: for example, orders for new tapes were taking as long as three to four weeks to be delivered, and he was resolved that CA would pay particular attention to giving a good service to the customer.

For some time, Engdata had been negotiating with a large British company for the retail marketing rights of a new magnetic digital tape which it had developed. It was claimed to be of a quality superior to any other comparable magnetic tape at present on the market. This company, which was hoping to sell these tapes directly to computer-manufacturers, did not wish to set up a retail organization to sell to computer-users. They were prepared, therefore, to grant CA exclusive selling rights within the UK, apart from sales to the computer-manufacturers which they would handle themselves. They had already been making audio tapes for a number of years. Since no specialized production equipment was needed for digital tapes, it would be possible to adjust the product mix between audio and digital tapes according to demand and at relatively short notice. This arrangement would be highly satisfactory for CA, since it would provide the company with a developed new product with which to commence operations in a market which was expanding rapidly. Furthermore, because of the ease with which their supplier could adjust his production schedules, CA could be assured of adequate supplies without having to make any long-term ordering commitments. This would provide CA with a great deal of flexibility in the early months, during which it was difficult to assess the level of sales likely to be achieved.

Technical Features of the New Magnetic Tape

Magnetic tape consists of a base to provide physical strength upon which the electrically sensitive material, small particles of ferrous oxide, is deposited. The ferrous oxide particles are retained and

bonded to the base by a plastic material. It was claimed by the makers that novel features in the manufacturing processes of the new tape were responsible for the following improved characteristics:
1. *Long Life.* The improved technical properties gave the tapes an increased resistance to wear. Without results from prolonged usage, it was not possible to give any firm estimate of how much longer they were likely to last compared with other makes, although it was possible to quote the results of a series of simulated high rate of wear abrasive tests which had been carried out. After these tests, 60% of the active deposit remained on the new tape, whereas only 20–30% was left on the other makes of tape tested. Although these figures could not be used directly as a measure of tape life, they did indicate the probability of a considerable improvement over existing tapes.
2. *Equipment Wear.* Magnetic-tape wear resulted in the liberation of highly abrasive particles of ferrous oxide which were deposited in the user equipment, thereby contributing to its wear. Reduction in tape wear could be expected to reduce the equipment wear with consequent benefits from lowered maintenance and repair costs which could be very high. Again, it was not possible to quantify this gain, but Mr Ainsworth thought that it could be made a significant selling point.
3. *Lower 'Drop-Outs' of Data.* All magnetic tapes occasionally suffered from a partial loss of the data stored in them; when a 'drop-out', as this was called, occurred it was necessary to reconstitute the information stored on the tape. The new tape, which had better data-retention, would enable a higher rate of data throughput due to a reduction in the time required for reconstitution after drop-outs.

Pricing

Because of the absence of strong competition there had been no pressure on profit margins, and Engdata considered that the prices currently being charged for magnetic tapes were unduly high. It seemed likely, therefore, that CA would be able to undercut its competitor's prices by a significant amount should it wish to do so.

At that time, the price of a 2500 feet reel of $\frac{1}{2}$ in. magnetic tape varied appreciably with the volume bought. Representative prices being charged were:

3 Ms £18 per reel for 1 to 9 reels reducing to £15 for orders in excess of 500 reels.
ICT: £16 to £20 per reel.   IBM: £16 per reel.

The cost of tapes to CA was still being negotiated with the supplier, but Mr Ainsworth expected that it would be in the region of £10 per reel. He had no figures for the comparable costs to his competitors, but he felt sure that CA would have an advantage, since production costs were not likely to vary much between his supplier and its competitors, while the latter had to bear a 10% import duty. CA overhead costs could also be expected to be lower. Details of the CA budget for the first year, and breakeven charts at various selling prices, are given in Exhibits 8.3 and 8.4 respectively. Ainsworth deduced that he would be able to offer a substantial price advantage to his customers and still make a profit.

It could be argued that the quality of the tapes to be marketed by CA would justify a higher price, and that a low price might be interpreted by the buyers as showing lack of confidence in the quality claims. Ainsworth thought otherwise. He believed customers were sufficiently sophisticated to be able to judge the validity of the claims for themselves once they had gathered sufficient user experience. The problem was to persuade them to try the tapes in the first place, since the technical advantages were long term and could not be assessed from a short demonstration. A lower price would encourage them to make their initial purchase. Even a small price advantage could mean significant cost savings to a large user. Ainsworth knew of an insurance company which was setting up a library consisting of 500 tapes at a cost of £7500; even a price advantage of only 5% would reduce this cost by £375. On the other hand, he feared that if he set his price too low other manufacturers might make price reductions in retaliation, whereas they might ignore a small firm only undercutting them slightly in an expanding market.

Volume discount must also be considered; Mr Ainsworth had been advised that the size of the normal order was 100 tapes, and that the majority of sales would be in the range of 50–100 tapes. 3Ms were at present giving the following discounts:

Order Size	Price
1–9 reels	Basic
10–49 reels	Basic–7½%
50–499 reels	Basic–10%
Over 500 reels	Basic–17%

The discounts CA were considering were aimed at giving the maximum price advantage over 3Ms to orders within the range

50–499. The following discounts were being proposed:

Order Size	Price
1–9 reels	Basic
10–49 reels	Basic–5%
50–499 reels	Basic–15%
Over 500 reels	Basic–20%

Distribution

Because of the small sum of money he was allowed for his first year, Ainsworth was limited in the scale of the initial operation. He had budgeted for one assistant in addition to himself; they would both be working from their Slough headquarters. He intended to increase his selling staff as sales and earnings mounted. The 250 square feet of space he had been allocated in the Engdata office block would be adequate for both office accommodation and storage space, since it was possible to store a considerable number of reels of magnetic tape in a limited area.

He expected the majority of early sales to result from personal visits, at first by himself, and, later, as the scale of operations increased, by members of his staff. Fortunately, comprehensive information on computer installations in the UK was available from the bimonthly publication *Computer Survey*. From this, CA would be able to find out for all installations the name of the company using the computer, its location, the make and type of the computer, and the purpose for which it was being used. Utilizing this data, it was possible to plot their geographical distribution on a map. Although this information would be of great assistance, it was hoped, nevertheless, that the majority of initial contacts would arise from introductions made with the help of other Engdata companies. An introductory pack of five reels was being planned which Mr Ainsworth could carry with him in his car. He thought that it would not be too difficult to persuade customers to buy these small packs; once the first purchase had been made, the quality and price of the new tapes was expected to ensure repeat orders.

Orders which could not be delivered by car would be dispatched by post or passenger train. By maintaining an adequate stock of tapes in the store, all orders would be promptly satisfied. In this way, tapes should be received by the customers within a week of the order being placed. It was to be expected that repeat orders would be received by post as well as from personal visits to the customer. However, the importance of personal contact would not be overlooked, as the company became established, since regular visits were regarded as an essential part of the service CA would offer, apart from their importance in obtaining repeat orders.

Future Policy

In August 1965, Mr Ainsworth knew that a final decision must be made on the details of the CA pricing policy and marketing plan in the very near future. He believed the company had a potential for very rapid growth provided the right decisions were made initially. He must, however, look ahead and relate his current decision to his long-term objectives.

Exhibit 8.1 Computer Ancillaries Limited: Cumulative Totals of UK Computer Installations, 1955–65 (excluding Computers taken out of Service)

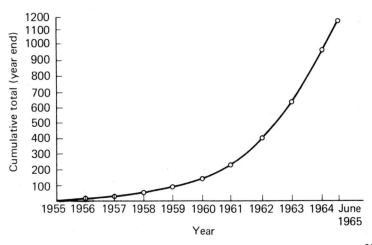

Exhibit 8.2 Computer Ancillaries Limited: Annual Deliveries of Computers to UK Users, 1955–65

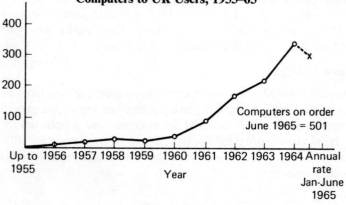

Exhibit 8.3 Computer Ancillaries Limited

1. Operational Budget, October 1965–October 1966

Salaries	£	£
J. Ainsworth + Assistant	5000	
Share of Secretary	500	
Pensions and NHI	500	
	——	6000
Accommodation		
250 ft² at £2 10s per ft²	625	
Rent of Furniture and Equipment	75	
	——	700
Staff Cars: Running and Depreciation		1000
Distribution		
Van and driver	1200	
Packaging	175	
Insurance	125	
	——	1500
Advertising		1500
Miscellaneous Expenses		
Stationery, postage, etc.	200	
Entertainment	500	
	——	700
Contingency		300
		——
		11 700

2. Capital Budget

Cars	1500
Stock	6000
	——
	£7500

Exhibit 8.4 Computer Ancillaries Limited: Breakeven Analysis at Different Selling Prices

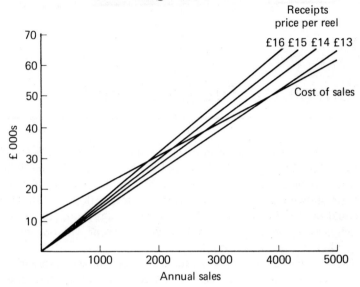

9

Convoluted Tubing Limited

Trevor Howard looked gloomily at the sheet of figures in front of him. 'John, this just won't do,' he said to his accountant, John Philpotts, 'our output is approaching the half million mark, and here we are showing a profit for the year which is little over £10 000. I could put my money in the Post Office Savings Bank and get as much income and none of the worry. What's wrong with our set up and what can we do about it?'

Convoluted Tubing had been established some fifteen years earlier by Trevor Howard, and had specialized in manufacturing convoluted hoses from seamless tubes. The business had been originally founded upon specialized stainless steel tubing for hoses used on high performance aircraft, and from this had been built up a high standard of know-how in the field. Because each convolution was individual and not put on spirally, the manufacture required very highly specialized machines, each capable of large volume output.

The manufacture of the convoluted tubing itself required the back-up of a large design team to deal with the individual customer requirements for end fittings, particularly in the high performance products. The remainder of the activity consisted of the manufacture of the fittings and the assembly of the complete hose ready for delivery to the customer. Over the years, the original market in the aircraft industry has been considerably extended to include hose used on machine tools, and similar items where flexible connections are required, and also for some domestic purposes. This had led to the manufacture of several different qualities of hose and fittings.

At the present time, the products fall into five product groups, each of which is sufficiently homogeneous to be considered as a single product. The present potential demand for each of the product groups is shown in Exhibit 9.1.

38

As a result of his meeting with Howard, John Philpotts examined each of the five product groups carefully, and produced the analysis of costs and selling price shown in Exhibit 9.2.

On the 11 February 1970, Howard called a meeting of some of his senior executives to discuss the problem. Present at this meeting were, besides Philpotts and Howard himself, Bill Bowden, the production manager and Maurice Denham, the sales manager.

Bill Bowden set the ball rolling by saying that the plant was fully stretched at the present time. All six machines were fully working and it would not be likely that the present 20 hours actual output per week achieved from each machine could be bettered. There were substantial setting up times and runs were on the whole small. The only way that output could be increased would be to put in new plant, but this was not possible in the existing premises.

'I have already explored the possibility of obtaining an industrial development certificate to expand on our present site,' Howard commented, 'but so far it is no go. The only way that we can get more room would be to move to a development area, and quite frankly, at my time of life, I am not going to uproot my family to move to the North-East or some similar area. We have just got to look at ways of making our existing operation profitable. What about the price situation, Maurice, is there any possibility that we could up our prices?'

'Quite frankly, Trevor,' Maurice Denham replied, 'I think that we are already at the top of the scale as far as price is concerned. I know that, at the present time, the potential sales are considerably in excess of our capacity and I continually have to liaise with Bill to make sure that we can reasonably cope with the orders that we take. But if we tried to put the price up to any significant extent, the Americans and Swedes would step up their deliveries to the UK at their old prices and we would be cut out. This would certainly be true as far as our high quality products are concerned. For the commercial grades we are already in competition with braided hose and other substitutes, and price changes would certainly upset this market.'

'How far do your men in the field specialize in their customers,' Howard asked Denham. 'It seems to me that we spread our net quite widely in trying to get business, and, in our present situation, perhaps we ought to be more selective in the way we employ our salesmen and direct the advertising policy. If we knew a little more about the profitability of our products, perhaps we could drop the less profitable ones, or at least not use expensive marketing resources to win business in those products.'

Bill Bowden followed this up by saying that he was at a Rotary Club meeting the previous week and had been talking to Jonathan Wilkes who managed an engineering plant on the same trading estate. Wilkes had been discussing the success he had had in organizing a 'half-shift' of local people in the evening. While, initially, the skills had been below par, these had been brought rapidly up to the standard of the day shift. Other people whom he had met at a local productivity group meeting organized by the British Productivity Council had had similar experiences. He felt that such a shift would, after the initial induction and training programme, improve the output of the plant by some 40% and on estimates that had been prepared for him would increase the 'fixed' element of his overheads by some £4000 per month.

The meeting concluded by Howard asking Philpotts to prepare a report setting out, first, the most desirable product mix for the company to sell, and the effect that this would have upon profitability, and, second, the implications of the proposal made by Bill Bowden for starting up an evening 'half-shift'.

The balance sheet and profit and loss account for the company for the year to 31 December 1969 are shown in Exhibits 9.3 and 9.4.

An analysis of the production times shows that, on average, each unit requires the following times on the convoluting machine:

Product group A	18 min
Product group B	36 min
Product group C	42 min
Product group D	30 min
Product group E	24 min.

In addition, there was the cost of manufacture of the fittings and assembly of the complete unit. Surplus requirements above capacity were subcontracted out to local machine shops.

Exhibit 9.1 Convoluted Tubing Limited
Estimated Potential Demand by Product Groups

Product Group	Demand (Units) per Month
A	700
B	950
C	150
D	900
E	300

Exhibit 9.2 Convoluted Tubing Limited
Unit Costs and Selling Prices by Groups

Product Group	Total Cost £	Variable Cost £	Selling Price £
A	26	18	30
B	35	28	40
C	72	52	85
D	20	15	30
E	18	14	30

Exhibit 9.3 Convoluted Tubing Limited
Balance Sheet as at 31 December 1969

	£	£
Fixed Assets		
Buildings at Cost		38 821
Plant and Equipment, at Cost	127 746	
Less Depreciation	52 310	
		75 436
Vehicles at Cost	6340	
Less Depreciation	3920	
		2420
Dies and Tools at Valuation		19 000
		135 677
Insurance Policy on Life of Mr Howard		12 720
(Surrender Value £11 500)		
Current Assets		
Stocks and Work in Progress	27 920	
Debtors	86 720	
Marketable Securities (Market Value £16 210)	13 740	
Cash in Hand and at Bank	19 240	
		147 620
		296 017

Current Liabilities

Creditors	72 684	
Accrued Liabilities	6340	
Tax Due	7210	
Dividends	5000	
		91 234
		204 783
Owing on Hire Purchase		37 630
Net Assets		£167 153

Share Capital

Authorized—100 000 £1 Ordinary Shares	100 000
Issued 90 000 £1 Ordinary Shares	90 000
Retained Profits	21 233
	111 233
Tax Due 1 January 1971	5920
Mortgage Secured on Freehold Factory	50 000
	£167 153

Exhibit 9.4 Convoluted Tubing Limited
Profit and Loss Account for the Year to 31 December 1969

	£	£
Sales		469 680
Cost of Goods Sold		
Materials	142 740	
Direct Labour	55 870	
Variable Overheads (Factory)	94 766	
Fixed Overheads (Factory)	90 600	
		383 976
		85 704
Selling and Administrative Expenses		75 040
Net Profit		£10 664

10

The Expanding Company Limited (B)

At their monthly board meeting, held on 20 November 1968, the board of directors of Feldmans (Industrial Bankers) Limited authorized the plan for the expansion of The Expanding Company Limited into the Midland region (see page 13). The factory premises and regional office were established in the early months of 1969 and a number of small contracts were obtained both for the factory units and for ordinary civil engineering work.

In September 1969, the company was invited to tender for a major civil engineering contract concerned with the provision of roads, services, and other development work in connection with the redevelopment of the Birmingham region. At their monthly management meeting on 28 November, Mr Willis and some of his senior executives were considering the tender and other details that had been drawn up for this contract prior to submitting the tender the following week. Because of its relative size, Mr Willis was anxious that this contract should meet the profitability levels that had been forecast in the figures on which the expansion had been approved. He was also uneasy because recent difficulties encountered by other companies in the region, allied with the untried nature of his new management team in the region, could well give the impression that the company might not meet the completion date. It was agreed, therefore, that the contract should still meet the profitability performance required for civil engineering work, even though it might overrun by three months.

The schedule of forecast expenditures and claims relating to the contract is given in Exhibit 10.1. Labour costs are expected to be met in the month in which they are incurred; materials and other expenses in the month following that in which they are incurred;

claims will be submitted monthly in the month following that in which the work is done and to be paid, less 10% retention, in the next month. Retention monies outstanding at the end of the contract should be cleared within the following three months and can be taken in equal instalments in each of those months.

Plant specific to the contract will be required. This will be purchased as to £50 000 in the first month and £60 000 in the fifth month. It is expected that this plant will realize some £20 000 on completion of the contract.

Exhibit 10.1 The Expanding Company Limited

Schedule of Expenditure and Income for New Contract

Month	Labour, etc. £	Materials and Other £	Claims Submitted £
1	2000	130 000	—
2	4000	195 000	146 000
3	5000	180 000	220 000
4	10 000	170 000	209 000
5	20 000	190 000	203 000
6	25 000	100 000	234 000
7	30 000	120 000	140 000
8	30 000	140 000	166 000
9	32 000	160 000	184 000
10	28 000	150 000	214 000
11	18 000	100 000	198 000
12	16 000	80 000	140 000
13	24 000	60 000	106 000
14	24 000	51 000	93 000
15	18 000	10 000	84 000
16	12 000	2000	30 000
17	8000	2000	16 000
18	3000	1000	12 000
19	—	—	5000

11

Corfair Industrial Services Limited

Charles Gardner is currently looking at the future financial requirements of the business in view of the plans that the board recently approved in principle. These plans will provide for the expansion of the firm's activities by some 25% over the next three years, with the consequential increase in working capital and new investment in fixed assets.

As a preliminary to his review of the position, he has before him the recently published accounts for the company. These show that the net assets employed by the company increased from £8 890 000 at 31 March 1968 to £10 928 000 at 31 March 1969 (see Exhibit 11.1). At the same time, the retained profits for the year had only increased to some £210 000 (see Exhibit 11.2) and, although he was aware that the company had raised £1 569 000 convertible loan stock during the year, less expenses connected with the issue of £65 000, he felt that he should be more aware of the way the sources and uses of funds had changed during the year. Accordingly, he called in his personal assistant, who had recently returned from a year's course in management studies, and asked him to prepare for the board's consideration an analysis of the changes for the year to 31 March 1969.

Being on his mettle to show that his recently awarded DMS would be a good investment, his assistant took away a set of the accounts and began his perusal of the balance sheets and profit and loss accounts, together with the notes included in the published figures (see Exhibit 11.3).

Question
Assuming that you were Charles Gardner's personal assistant, how would you prepare the required statement?

Exhibit 11.1 Corfair Industrial Services Limited
Group Accounts for the Year to 31 March

	1969 £ 000s	1968 £ 000s
Fixed Assets		
Net Book Value (See Note 3, Exhibit 11.3)	9094	8125
Goodwill	—	412
Subsidiary Company not Consolidated	85	—
Trade Investments	234	42
Current Assets		
Stocks and Work in Progress	3468	2642
Debtors and Payments in Advance	2597	2065
Investment Grants Receivable	278	165
Deposits at Short Call	75	110
Cash and Bank Balances	76	94
	6494	5076
	15 907	13 655
Current Liabilities		
Bank Overdrafts	2788	2342
Creditors and Accrued Liabilities	1342	1598
Taxation—Current	537	513
Final Ordinary Dividend	312	312
	4979	4765
	£10 928	£8890
Issued Capital		
5s Ordinary Shares	4453	4453
Capital Reserves	423	435
Revenue	1973	1763
	6849	6651
Interest of Minority Shareholders	1210	939
5¼% Debenture Loan 1978/82	1300	1300
9½% Convertible Unsecured Loan Stock 1986/89	1569	—
	£10 928	£8890

Exhibit 11.2 Corfair Industrial Services Limited
Group Profit and Loss Accounts for the Year to 31 March

			1969	1968
			£ 000s	£ 000s
Sales			17 986	16 842
Operating Profit (See Note 1, Exhibit 11.3)			1315	1210
Taxation (See Note 2, Exhibit 11.3)			537	513
After Tax Profit			778	697
Minority Interests			123	113
Profits Available to Shareholders			655	584
Dividends				
Ordinary Shares: Interim 3%	133			133
Final 7%	312			312
			445	445
Retained from Year's Profits			£210	£139

Exhibit 11.3 Corfair Industrial Services Limited
Notes to the Accounts for the Year to 31 March 1969

1. The operating profit is after dealing with:

	1969	1968
	£ 000s	£ 000s
Depreciation	3841	2932
Pension Fund Contribution	65	62
Debenture Interest	68	68
Convertible Loan Stock Interest	74	—
Interest on Overdraft	196	161
Audit Fees	8	6
Directors' Emoluments	18	18
Investment Income	(32)	(10)
Interest Received	(7)	(8)

2. Taxation on profits for the year:

	1969	1968
Corporation Tax 45% (42½%)	540	511
Adjustments in Respect of Previous Years	(3)	2
	537	513

3. Fixed Assets (figures in £ 000s):

(a) *Assets*	Freehold and Leasehold Properties	Plant and Machinery	Vehicles and Mobile Plant	Fixtures and Fittings
Cost or at Valuation at 1.4.68	1842	11 165	2627	396
Additions (Net of Investment Grants)	—	3417	920	15
Revaluation at 30.6.68	500	—	—	—
	2342	14 582	3547	411
Disposals	—	142	23	2
Balance at 31.3.69	2342	14 440	3524	409
(b) *Depreciation*				
Balance at 1.4.68	146	5729	1781	249
Accumulated Depreciation on Assets Disposed of	—	115	8	2
	146	5614	1773	247
Depreciation for Year	54	2880	881	26
	200	8494	2654	273
Net Book Value	2142	5946	870	136

Depreciation is provided for by way of an annual charge based upon a percentage of the original cost, ranging from 5% to 25% depending upon the type of asset.

4. Movements in reserves:

	1969 £ 000s	1968 £ 000s
Capital		
Balance at 1.4.68	435	447
Surplus on Revaluation of Buildings	500	—
Goodwill written off	(412)	—
Expenses of Convertible Stock Issue	(65)	—
Loss on Sale of Fixed Assets	(35)	(12)
Balance at 31.3.69	423	435
Revenue		
Balance at 1.4.68	1763	1624
Increase in Retained Profits	210	139
	1973	1763

5. Investment Grants:

Grants are receivable on some of the Company's plant. The amount shown in the balance sheet represents the amounts receivable in respect of the past year's purchases.

12

Supershops Limited

John Makin has, over the past 15 years, built up a small chain of specialized high-class shops which have been very successful. For some time, he has not increased the number of shops because to do so in his own specialized field would have meant expanding the geographical area of operations too widely for him to maintain good management control.

He has recently been approached to see if he would be interested in acquiring a store, on a good site near to his centre of operations, which could be used for selling a range of products not competitive with his other shops. The rent of the store would be £3000 per annum payable half-yearly on 1 January and 1 July on a tenancy with 20 years to run, and for which a premium of £12 500 would be required.

Converting the premises to his requirements would cost some £14 300, of which £6800 would be in respect of fixtures and fittings which would be depreciated over 10 years. In addition, he would need a van for deliveries which would cost £800 and be depreciated over 4 years.

Taking into account the position of the premises and his estimate of the potential trade available in the area, Makin estimates that for each of the product groups sold, turnover would be as follows for the first year:

Product Group A £5000 per month Jan.–Aug., thereafter £7000
Product Group B £20 000 per month Jan.–Aug., thereafter £30 000
Product Group C £10 000 per month Jan.–May, thereafter £15 000

The goods are purchased from suppliers who give one month's credit at prices which would give the following discounts on retail prices:

Group A 30%   Group B 15%   Group C 20%

Mr Makin would require a minimum of two months' stock of all goods sold to be maintained at all times.

The costs of running the store are estimated as follows:

1. Fixed overheads (including rent and depreciation of fixtures and van): £15 880.
2. Wages and salaries Jan.–April: £2000 per month
   May–July: £3000 per month
   Aug.–Dec.: £4000 per month
3. Other variable overheads: 5% of sales value.

It is estimated that cash sales will be at the rate of £8000 per month throughout the year. The remainder of sales will be on a credit basis and the average time it will take to collect the sums due from customers will be two months.

Questions

As financial adviser to Mr Makin you have been asked:

1. Is the store likely to make a profit in the first year?
2. What capital will be needed to support operations in this year?
3. What alternative sources of funds are available to Mr Makin to reduce the burden on his cash resources?
4. How would the balance sheet appear at the end of the first year's trading?

13

Grange Sportswear

Grange Sportswear was an old-established company which specialized in the distribution of sportswear and sports equipment. It operated through a central warehouse situated in Glasgow and from four regional depots. Over the years, a number of international links had been established both in the distribution of clothing and equipment to overseas territories—particularly the Commonwealth—and importing equipment of foreign manufacture, principally from the USA and Italy, for distribution within the UK.

With the greater spending power of the young who, on the whole, were more athletically inclined than their elders, and with the stimulus to greater participation in sports generated by television and the ease of foreign travel, the business had made steady, if unspectacular, progress during the 'fifties.

The company had for many years banked with the Scottish Land Bank who had occasionally made very modest overdraft facilities available. These had proved adequate to finance expansion until accumulated profits build up sufficiently to provide all the funds required. For the last three years, no use had been made at all of bank borrowing except for a period in the early spring each year when the new seasons goods were bought in to cope with the rush of orders that was traditionally received in the early summer.

Early in 1960, the company negotiated with a local authority to purchase a new warehouse and ancillary facilities in the south-west of England—an area where, hitherto, it had not been represented. It was estimated that the costs of setting up the warehouse would be of the order of £52 000. Fred Good, the merchandizing manager of Grange, estimated that the extension would boost the sales of the company from its recent level of £370 000 to £455 000 in the first year and £500 000 in subsequent years.

In preparation for their discussion with the bank, Good and Eric Knight, the managing director, had prepared a schedule showing the balance sheets and profit and loss accounts for the last two years and a forecast of the present year's figures (see Exhibit 13.1). In view of the likely growth in retained profits that would result from the expansion, it was felt that if the company could borrow £50 000 to cover the initial set up of the new warehouse the company would be able to pay it off over a three year period. After some discussion with the local manager and his head office, the bank finally agreed to the loan which was to be on an overdraft basis and to bear interest at 2% above bank rate.

The company managed to bring the new warehouse on stream in time to catch the tail end of the market for summer sports; it was in full-scale operation by the autumn.

While he was holidaying in Dorset, the bank manager took the opportunity of meeting Fred Good, who was on one of his periodic visits to the warehouse, and of looking over the premises and seeing how it operated. He was quite impressed by this visit and reported very favourably upon it to his head office when he returned. Once or twice, he met Eric Knight at local functions in Glasgow, and was pleased to learn that the growth in sales was matching up to the expectation upon which the expansion was based.

Late in February 1961 he received the following letter from Eric Knight together with a copy of the company's accounts for the previous year:

Dear Mr Gallagher,

Alice has asked me to thank you and your wife for the flowers which you sent her in hospital. It was indeed kind of you to send your good wishes in this way. We are expecting her home next week.

Fred Good told me that you were quite impressed by our new warehouse when you were in Dorset during the summer. In fact, things seem to have turned out better than we thought. Sales have exceeded what we were forecasting by a handsome margin with a consequent improvement in the profit position. Copies of our accounts for the year to 31 December last are enclosed for your records.

Yours sincerely,
Eric Knight

Exhibit 13.1 Grange Sportswear

Balance Sheets as at 31 December

		1958		1959		1960
		(Actual)		(Actual)		(Esti-mated)
		£		£		£
Fixed Assets						
At Cost		121 300		134 800		187 500
Less Depreciation		74 800		87 400		94 600
		46 500		47 400		92 900
Current Assets						
Stock	63 400		69 300		82 400	
Debtors	93 700		91 400		112 800	
Cash in Hand	3200		4100		3200	
		160 300		164 800		198 400
		206 800		212 200		291 300
Current Liabilities						
Creditors	51 600		48 500		58 900	
Accrued Expenses	6400		2900		3000	
Provision for						
Taxation	14 200		20 400		17 900	
Dividends (Net)	4600		4900		4900	
		76 800		76 700		84 700
		£130 000		£135 500		£206 600
Share Capital						
(Ordinary Shares)		80 000		80 000		80 000
Capital Reserve		1100		1100		1100
Retained Profits		28 500		36 500		53 400
		109 600		117 600		134 500
Future Taxation		20 400		17 900		30 500
		130 000		135 500		165 000
Funds Required						41 600
		£130 000		£135 500		£206 600

Profit and Loss Accounts for the Years to 31 December

	1958	1959	1960
			(Esti-
	(Actual)	(Actual)	mated)
	£	£	£
Sales	349 600	372 500	455 700
Cost of Goods Sold	227 400	249 300	297 900
Gross Profit	122 200	123 200	157 800
Total Operating Expenses	83 700	87 500	100 600
Trading Profit	38 500	35 700	57 200
Profits and Income Tax	20 400	17 900	30 500
Profits after Tax	18 100	17 800	26 700
Dividends 20% Less Tax	9200	9800	9800
Retained Profits	£8900	£8000	£16 900

Exhibit 13.2 Grange Sportswear

Actual Balance Sheet as at 31 December 1960

		£
Fixed Assets		
At Cost		196 400
Less Depreciation		95 100
		101 300
Current Assets		
Stock	174 800	
Debtors	262 100	
Cash in Hand	1100	
		438 000
		539 300
Current Liabilities		
Bank Overdraft	53 300	
Owing on HP	21 200	
Creditors	248 300	
Accrued Expenses	17 600	
Provision for Taxation	17 900	
Dividends	14 700	
		373 000
		£166 300

Share Capital (Ordinary Shares)	80 000
Capital Reserve	1100
Retained Profit	52 100
	133 200
Future Taxation	33 100
	£166 300

Actual Profit and Loss Account for Year to 31 December 1960

Sales	484 400
Costs of Goods Sold	318 500
Gross Profit	165 900
Total Operating Expenses	102 500
Trading Profit	63 400
Profits and Income Tax	33 100
Profits after Tax	30 300
Dividends 30% Less Tax	14 700
Retained Profits	£15 600

14

Levy Hardware Limited*

In December 1965, the Dorchester Investment Trust was considering acquiring a financial interest in the Levy Hardware Company Limited. Talbot Esmond, a director of the Dorchester Investment Trust, reviewed the information he had obtained from Mr Levy and his accountants. This information included notes from the meetings as well as financial and production data.

Note on Meeting in Cork, Eire, on 9 November 1965

Present: R. Levy (managing director)

J. Roxton (Blue Hill and Company, Chartered Accountants)

Talbot Esmond (Dorchester Investment Trust)

1. Levy is a man of around 55 who has had a considerable experience in Australia in the electronics industry. He is clearly a man who is very ingenious with his hands. He has designed a new kind of light switch which operates on a press-button basis, and which has considerable advantages over conventional light switches.

The installation advantage is, however, much more interesting. A Levy switch can be inserted in a wall within five minutes. A conventional switch can take anything up to 40 minutes to install. Levy's switch requires no electrical connections. It operates on a magnetic dry reed relay, and is held in position by magnetic attraction to the electrical conduits behind the wall. Levy claims the installation costs are less than on conventional switches because no recess is required in the wall and there are considerable

*Case material of the Management Case Research Unit, Cranfield, Bedford, England, and prepared as a basis for class discussion. This case was made possible through the cooperation of a British company which remains anonymous. Reproduced by kind permission of the Cranfield School of Management.

savings in conduit cutting and plastering and in the saving of a switch box. Since a modern house has an average of eight switches, Levy has clearly a substantial market if he can persuade architects and house-developers to use his Magna-Switches.

2. Levy has been trying to promote his company for the last two years. His first year was taken up with obtaining capital and persuading various manufacturers to make the relay for his Magna-Switch. All his parts are bought in, but it has taken him a long time to develop a complete range of switches. To sell his product effectively, it is necessary to have compatible designs for living rooms, kitchens, bathrooms and lavatories.

Levy has borrowed some £18 000 from the Credit Company of Cork. The money has been put into his company on an un-secured basis, but in the event of failure of the company the Credit Company will be entitled to the patents on Levy's switch device. He claims to have patents throughout the world. Should the company succeed, the Credit Company can convert its loan into 26% of the ordinary share capital of the company.

The current position is that the company has made in its operations to date a loss of some £6000, of which £2000 was incurred in the year ending 30 April 1965. Currently there is a shortage of capital because Levy has tied up most of the money which he has put into the company in parts and stocks of switches. He has been operating the company on a one-man basis and, quite clearly, he has been very stretched trying to do everything. He has made a number of mistakes; in particular he has failed to sell his product.

To date, Levy has sold some 10 000 units in 14½ months; 1500 of these have been sold to one buyer in Belgium. While Levy has been able to interest a number of UK firms, he has not really obtained any large orders. The reason for this has been that he had only recently completed his full range of switches: his policy of having the parts fabricated and plated in the UK has obviously caused considerable delay. Furthermore, it has involved Levy himself in waste of his own management time. On this point, it will be necessary to question whether Levy is right to try to set up his operation in Cork. There may be tax advantages and it may have been necessary for him to raise the initial cash from the Credit Company there, but his markets are mainly the UK and Europe: he intends to sell nothing in Cork.

3. Levy currently occupies a small warehouse space in Cork. His overheads are low and he has no production line for assembling his parts. When he obtains an order he brings in a few women to assemble sufficient packages to meet the order. At the moment, he obviously has far too much money tied up in unsold stock. At his present cost level, he would breakeven selling 12 000 units per annum; he has the capacity to assemble 25 000 units per annum. Levy claims that at current cost he is selling his switches at a net profit per unit of $22\frac{1}{2}\%$.

4. Levy is seeking some £35 000 to expand his operation. He needs salesmen in the UK and he would like to put his company on a proper production basis. While Levy himself might be able to handle the assembly and design side of his product in Cork, he is quite incapable of selling and marketing the product in the UK.

   It should be possible to either eliminate the Credit Company by paying it off or to retain its support and persuade the company to put up additional cash. Whether to retain the Credit Company or not would depend upon whether it was decided that it was a commercial proposition to assemble and manufacture in Eire.

   Currently, parts are obtained from Wales Electronics and plating is done by Charlotte's of Brighton.

   Blue Hill and Company, Levy's chartered accountants, have agreed to submit a scheme showing how the £35 000 will be spent.

5. When the scheme has been received, Dorchester will reply in principle setting out the basis on which an investment would be considered in Levy Hardware. The basis would depend upon the profits anticipated from the company and would be related to the capital necessary to achieve those profits. Furthermore, it was pointed out to Levy that he had not sufficient management experience to give Dorchester confidence that he could run the company as it expanded. It was agreed that Dorchester would provide considerable management assistance to the company if the scheme proceeded and that Levy would accept Dorchester's management recommendations. 11 November 1965.

Mr Esmond reviewed this information, as well as the financial and production information shown in Exhibits 14.1 to 14.11.

Exhibit 14.1

Blue Hill and Company,   6, Franklin Place,
Chartered Accountants.   Cork.
Talbot Esmond, Esq.,
Dorchester Investment Trust.   7 October 1965.
Dear Mr Esmond,

Levy Hardware Limited

We have pleasure in enclosing herewith a copy of the accounts of Levy Hardware Limited, for the year ended 30 April 1965.

You will note that there is a trading loss of £1952 for the year, but you are aware that this arises because of lack of turnover. A satisfactory rate of gross profit has been earned on sales, but, of course, at the level of turnover which was available in the year ended 30 April 1965 a profit would not be possible.

In the balance sheet, the tools have been shown at original cost and have not been depreciated. Mr Levy is of the opinion that no depreciation is required as the number of items produced has been so small.

The current market value of the patents and trademarks, of course, greatly exceeds the balance sheet value.

Mr Levy has discussed with us the proposal that you take an interest in the company. When the terms of this interest are being discussed, it will be necessary to put a value on the company as it stands. The two crucial issues in valuing the company are the valuation of the patents and trademarks and the valuation of goodwill. It is difficult to estimate the sum that should be included to cover development work and expenditure which Mr Levy incurred both before and since the setting up of this company. He has brought the project to the stage at which it is ready to go into full-scale production. The snags have been ironed out and the groundwork has been done, and all that remains is for sufficient capital to be available to go into production of the full range. The valuation of the goodwill belonging to the company at this point is difficult to determine, but it is a substantial figure. Likewise it is difficult to say what is the market value of the patents and trademarks. Mr Levy has no doubt that they have a substantial market value now, particularly in the U.S. and Canada.

Taking into account all of these factors, we suggest that the shares of the company are at present worth not less than £10 per share, but, as we mentioned above, it is difficult to put a firm value on them.

We have suggested to Mr Levy that there should be a meeting as soon as possible between your company and Mr Levy and ourselves so as to see if it is possible to reach a basis of agreement. We would suggest that some of the points to be discussed might be as follows:

1. Valuation of the company before issue of shares to Dorchester Investment Trust.
2. Type of shareholding to be held by Dorchester Investment Trust. Whether this holding should be interest bearing redeemable preference shares or whether it should be non-interest bearing ordinary shares in the company, or both.
3. Position of the Cork Credit Company in any negotiations for a new arrangement.

59

4. Question of appointment of directors by your company and the question of future dividend policy of the company.
5. The question of future policy regarding floatation of sale or merger. On this point, it will be necessary to reach an agreement which will be acceptable to Mr Levy.

In your agreement with the McLellan Construction Company, you have a clause whereby either party can give notice to the other party and buy them out unless they are themselves bought out. Mr Levy has already indicated to you that such an agreement would be unacceptable to him, and we are in agreement with him that it would not be a reasonable clause.

We look forward to hearing from you as to what lines your proposition may take and we would like to see a meeting arranged as soon as possible.

Yours faithfully,
Seaver P. Columbia,
Blue Hill and Company.

Exhibit 14.2 Levy Hardware Limited

Report of the Directors

The Directors submit their report and statement of accounts of the company for the year ended 30 April 1965.

The loss amounted to	£1953
To this has been added balance of loss from previous year	£4257
Loss carried forward to next year	£6210

No amount has been carried to reserve and no dividend is recommended.

The company has had an encouraging year's trading, and there has not been any change in the nature of the company's business during the year.

In accordance with Section 160 of the Companies Act, 1963, Blue Hill and Company will continue in office as auditors.

On behalf of the Board,
R. Levy Director.

Exhibit 14.3 Levy Hardware Limited
Report of the Auditors to the Members of Levy Hardware Limited

In my opinion, the attached balance sheet and profit and loss account give a true and fair view of the state of the Company's affairs at 30 April 1965, and of the Company's loss for the year ended on that date.

I have obtained all the information and explanations which I consider necessary. In my opinion, the Company has kept proper books of account so far as appears from my examination of those books; and the balance sheet and profit and loss account, which are in agreement with the books, comply with the Companies Act, 1963.

Seaver P. Columbia
Chartered Accountant

5 October 1965.   Blue Hill and Company

Exhibit 14.4 Levy Hardware Limited

Trading and Profit and Loss Accounts for the Year Ended 30 April 1965

8½ months to 30.4.64				
£			£	£
3926	Sales			3994
—	*Deduct:* Stock of Raw Materials 1 May 1964		1352	
5317	Add Purchases		1589	
	Freight Inwards		116	
			3057	
1352	Less Closing Stock of Raw Materials		1680	
3965	Materials Used		1377	
1274	Wages and Salaries		817	
5239			2194	
	Adjust: Stock of Partly Manufactured Goods at Start	1829		
1829	Stock of Partly Manufactured Goods at End	1755	74	
3410			2268	
	Adjust: Stock of Finished Goods at start	181		
181	Stock of Finished Goods at End	151		
			30	
3229	Cost of Goods Sold			2298
697	Gross Profit			1697
	Deduct overhead expenses			
666	Salaries		565	
470	Rent		364	
193	Insurance		53	
36	Light, Heat, and Power		47	
225	Printing and Stationery		74	
126	Postage, Telegrams, and Telephone		111	
13	Bank Charges		21	
22	Subscriptions		20	
197	Patent Renewal Fees		—	
36	Packing Materials		20	
84	Freight Outwards		104	
730	Advertising		365	
98	Commission		152	

249	Legal Expenses	—
772	Travel and Motor Expenses	462
65	Auditor's Remuneration	65
—	Secretarial Services	101
286	General Expenses	66
687	Interest Charges	957
—	Repairs and Maintenance	14
	Depreciation:	
—	Equipment and Tools	57
—	Furniture and Office Equipment	31

| 4955 | | 3649 |

| 4258 | Net Loss | 1952 |

Submitted by Blue Hill and Company, 5 October 1965.

Exhibit 14.5 Levy Hardware Limited

Profit and Loss Appropriation Account for the Year Ended 30 April 1965

8½ months
to 30.4.64

| — | Balance 1 May 1964 | 4258 |
| 4258 | Add Net Loss for year | 1952 |

| 4258 | Balance Carried to Balance Sheet | 6210 |

Submitted by Blue Hill and Company, 5 October 1965.

Exhibit 14.6 Levy Hardware Limited

Balance Sheet as at 30 April 1965

30 April 1964	*Capital Employed*	Authorized	Issued
	Share Capital and Reserves		
7400	at £1 each	10 000	7400
4258	Profit and Loss Account		(6210)
3142			1190
15 000	Loans from Credit Company		18 000
18 142			19 190

	Employment of Capital	Original	Deprecia- tion to	Net
	Fixed Assets	Cost	Date	Value
4275	Dies	5095	–	5095
558	Equipment and Tools	566	57	509
217	Furniture and Office Equipment	312	31	281
7749	Patents and Trademarks	8652		8652
	(Renewal Fees have been			
12 799	Capitalized)	14 625	88	14 537
	Current Assets			
3363	Stocks and Work in Progress		3587	
319	Debtors		385	
303	Prepayments and Deposits		90	
2945	Cash at Bank		1673	
23	Cash in Hand		6	
6953	*Less Current Liabilities*		5741	
1610	Creditors and Accrued Expenses		1088	
5343				4653
18 142				19 190

On Behalf of the Board, R. Levy, Director.
Submitted by Blue Hill and Company, 5 October 1965.

Exhibit 14.7 Levy Hardware Limited

Blue Hill and Company   6, Franklin Place,
Chartered Accountants.   Cork.

Talbot Esmond, Esq.,
Dorchester Investment Trust.   17 November 1965

Dear Mr Esmond,

I thank you for your letter and I enclose herewith schedule of requirements in connection with the amount of £35 000 which it is envisaged would be necessary in the short term to reach reasonable production figures.

We are assuming that, provided stocks of switches could be built up, sales and production figures of 5000 sets per month would be reached in a short period. In fact, the only limiting factor in reaching this figure would be the building up of sufficient stocks in Cork to avoid hold-ups due to lack of parts. We set out on attached schedule projected annual figures, assuming production of 5000 switches per month. You will see that, on this basis, we have projected a breakeven, but, of course, the selling expenses at 5000 switches per month are extremely high.

If sales and production were increased to 10 000 switches per month, the gross profit would increase proportionately, and the administrative and selling overheads would tend to remain relatively fixed. The principal overhead alteration would be payment of commissions to the sales staff. It would be envisaged that they would not receive any commission on top of their salary at the rate of 5000 per month, but that commission might commence thereafter.

With the production at 10 000 per month, there should be a gross profit of over £40 000 available, and with production at 15 000 per month, there would be a gross profit of something over £60 000. In both cases, very little of the additional gross profit would be absorbed by additional overheads. Consequently, the profitability of the undertaking hinges on volume.

We enclose a projected balance sheet of the company, i.e., net assets required with production at 5000 switches per month and sales at £57 000 per annum. It is envisaged that production and sales could rise to 10 000 sets per month without any increase in the stock of parts, but that any further increase in production would require an increase in parts stock. Sales and production at the rate of 15 000 sets per month might require a stock of parts of roughly £20 000.

We have calculated debtors at an average of two months' credit and creditors, likewise, an average of two months' credit. With regard to debtors, the company gives a 10% cash discount for payment within 30 days. The sale price taken in our projected figure of 19s per set is net after allowance of the 10% cash discount.

All of these figures have been calculated assuming that only assembly will be carried out by the company. As you are aware, it is desirable that the company should build its own factory and manufacture the parts which are at present being bought in from other manufacturers.

We look forward to receiving your proposals for investment in the company on the basis that you would provide immediate working capital of, say, £35 000, and also your proposals as to what would be the position if your company were prepared to provide say an additional £50 000 in connection with the building and equipment of factory premises.

Yours sincerely,

Seaver P. Columbia

Blue Hill and Company.

Exhibit 14.8 Levy Hardware Limited

Projected Net Assets Position Assuming Production of 5000 Magna-Switches per Month

	£	£
Fixed Assets		
Amount per Balance Sheet at 30 April 1965		14 500
Add Additional Tools		4500
		19 000
Current Assets		
Stock of Parts for 20 000 Switches	16 000	
Debtors (Average Two Months)	10 000	26 000
		45 000
Deduct Creditors		
(Average Two Months and Taking into Account Building up of Stocks, Therefore, Purchases of 50 000 Approx.)		8000
Net Assets Required		37 000

Blue Hill and Company, 17 November 1965.

Exhibit 14.9 Levy Hardware Limited
Projected Annual Figures with Production of 5000 Magna-Switches per Month

Sales		£
60 000 per annum at 19s		57 000
Material Cost at 11s 6d	34 500	
Direct Labour Cost at 6d	1500	
	———	36 000
Administrative Costs		21 000
Salaries: Managing Director	3000	
1 Girl at £11 per Week		
1 Male at £14 per Week	1250	
Rent	600	
Rates	150	
Insurance	200	
Light, Heat, and Power	150	
Printing and Stationery	100	
Postage and Telephone	400	
Bank Charges	20	
Subscriptions	40	
Professional Fees	300	
Auditor's Remuneration	150	
Motor Expenses	400	
Other Items	250	
	———	7010
Selling Expenses		
Salaries: Sales Manager	2000 }	
2 Assistants at 1000	2000 } 4000	
Commissions	—	
Sales Staff Expenses—3 at 500	1500	
Freight Outwards	300	
Advertising	6500	
Other Items	250	
	———	12 550
Profit Before Tax		1440

Blue Hill and Company, 17 November 1965.

Exhibit 14.10 Levy Hardware Limited
Immediate Capital Requirements

	£
Stock of Parts 20 000 Switches Including Purchasing 10 000 Relays	15 000
Advertising: Technical Leaflet; Monthly Advertising Campaign	
to Builders and Architects; Magazines	6500
Tools and Dies	4500
Working Capital to provide for sales staff and other expenses in	
initial period. It is anticipated that it would take three to four	
months to build up sufficient stocks to operate at a level of	
5000 switches per month	9000
Blue Hill and Company, 17 November 1965.	£35 000

Exhibit 14.11 Levy Hardware Limited

Cost Per Switch (Components Only)

Costs Common to all Models	
Screw for Rem. Button	0·250
2 3/16 dis. Steel Bolts	2·659
2 Coil Springs	3·000
1 Coil Spring	0·750
Pad	0·246
Striker Plate	3·812
4 Screws	2·676
Packet	0·096
Instruction Sheet	2·110
Template	0·750
Box	3·659
Tool Charge	3·000
CIF Charges (freight inwards)	4·000
	27·008

Item	Emergency DE 400 S	Patio DPR 480	Universal DNDL 440	Marquise DMNDL 580	Passage DNL 300 S
Common Cost	27·008	27·008	27·008	27·008	27·008
Bolt	4·000	17·500	17·500	17·500	4·000
POY	28·000	28·000	28·000	33·000	28·000
Slide	18·000	18·000	18·000	18·000	12·000
Removable Button	9·000	9·000	9·000	9·000	8·100
Rod	3·000	3·000	3·000	3·000	—
Insert	4·480	—	—	—	—
Patio Inset and Seal	—	5·380	—	—	—
Dis. Device	—	—	20·000	—	—
Pin	—	—	—	60·000	—
Plating Charges	24·000	24·000	24·000	24·000	24·000
Total Parts Cost	117·488	131·888	146·508	191·508	103·108

Average Cost 138·100d = 11s 6d

	Emergency DE 400 S	Patio DPR 480	Universal DNDL 440	Marquise DMNDL 580	Passage DNL 300 S
Lowest Quantity Selling Price	17s 6d	19s 0d	20s 6d	26s 6d	12s 6d
Average Quantity Selling Price		19s 0d approximately			

15

Wendover Electronics Limited

Sam Bankwith put down the telephone receiver and made a note in his diary for Monday, 12 May 1969, 'Interview with Bank Manager—11.30,' and called in his financial controller John Welch. 'I have heard from Bedford's that we will most probably receive the Waveguide contract which we discussed the other week. It is about time we sorted out how we will finance the job when it arrives, and I have just arranged for us to see Wilkins at the bank a week on Monday. By that time, we should have received confirmation of the contract and be in a position to negotiate an extension to our overdraft. It would be as well if you could make some estimate of the amount by which our existing limits of £25 000 should be raised.'

Wendover had been started by Bankwith and two close associates some fifteen years before. They had been together at the Royal Aircraft Establishment in the early days of radar, and had worked with one of the major civilian contractors in the field for some years before setting up on their own.

The business was soundly based upon a product that had been developed by the directors. This was a tuning device used in radar and microwave equipment. In the first few years, manufacture had taken place in a small premises in South London employing little more than half a dozen people. In 1960, a small rented factory was secured and this proved adequate for the company's requirements until 1968. During 1968, the whole of the company's plant was moved to Crawley new town where spacious premises were rented which were more than adequate for the company's needs.

The directors had early pursued a policy of equipping their factory with the most modern automatic plant and 'clean rooms' for assembly work. It did mean, however, that the plant was capable of a much higher output than that currently achieved, this was evidenced by the high idle time for the major items of plant. It was to improve the machine utilization that Bankwith had, in recent months, visited a number of plants making sophisticated radar and similar equipment to see whether or not he could subcontract some of their work.

Whitehead (Brothers) Limited was a major firm in the industry, and had recently received a NATO contract for the supply of ground control radar. After extensive discussions with Charles Conroy, the managing director of Whiteheads, Bankwith had secured the offer of a contract for the manufacture and supply of 135 Waveguides and associated equipment at a price of £1500 each.

Demand for the tuning device had been good, but with no spectacular growth in recent years. In the first few months of the current year, the demand had been at the rate of approximately 100 per month at a price of £370 each. The costs of manufacture consisted of £44 per unit for direct materials and £96 for direct labour. Manufacturing overheads were running at the rate of £17 300 per month (this including substantial research and development expenditure as well as depreciation of £460). It is expected that output and sales of the tuning devices will continue at about the same rate for the rest of the year.

The proposed contract called for the manufacture of a test rig by the end of August 1969 which would cost £2500. This would be paid for by the customer and would cost approximately £800 in materials and £750 in direct labour. The delivery of the Waveguides would commence in October and was to be completed by the end of December; it was expected that the pattern of deliveries would be the same during the three month period.

The price of £1500 for the Waveguides was based upon the estimated costs of £276 each for direct materials, and £286 each for direct labour.

The manufacture of the test rig and the build-up of the labour force to meet the higher manufacturing activity during the period of the contract would add to the wage cost some £2000 in July and £5000 in August. Manufacture of the Waveguides would be virtually complete by the end of November, with only the test and inspection processes remaining to be done before delivery. If no additional work was secured before then, the labour force would be run down during December and would add some £4000 to the labour cost in that month.

The production cycle for the tuning devices lasted about one month and none were manufactured for stock but only to customers orders; they were delivered as soon as they passed inspection. It is expected, therefore, that the present level of work in progress for this product will remain unchanged. As far as possible, two months' materials would be kept in stock so as to avoid any delays through the non-availability of materials.

The materials for the Waveguide would be delivered entirely over the two month period from 1 August. The company made a practice of paying early those accounts where a cash discount could be obtained. Others were usually paid during the third month, so that, on average, accounts were paid two months after delivery. The additional work in progress was expected to average £45 000 over the period of the contract.

In common with other firms who supply the electronics industry, Wendovers had found difficulty in obtaining repayment within a reasonable time. Because of the drain on the company's funds that this entailed, Mr Bankwith had set up some years ago a small, but highly efficient, credit control section; as a result, he had managed to contain the debtors to the equivalent of two months' sales. In negotiating the contract, specific terms had been laid down that required payment by Whiteheads within two months of delivery, any amounts outstanding for longer being charged interest at 2% above bank rate. Bankwith was certain that amounts due would be collected within this two month period.

The manufacturing overheads were expected to increase to £30 000 per month during the three month manufacturing period. During August and December, the amounts would be £22 000 in each month.

Administration and selling expenses were normally about £3500 per month, but these were expected to increase to £5000 per month for the whole period from the beginning of August to the end of December.

Additional jigs and tools for the contract would cost £5000 and would be purchased in July. One item of machining may prove to be difficult on the company's existing plant, and it could prove necessary to purchase a more specialized machine tool for £15 000. If this was done, the existing machine would be sold in part exchange for £5000. It had cost £8000, when new, two years before.

Mr Bankwith had presumed that because the Waveguides would,

to a large extent, be exported, there would be no difficulty in obtaining bank finance. He was very disconcerted, therefore, when talking to Arthur Brown the manager of the local branch of the Eastchester Bank at a Rotary Club meeting, to be told that the clamp-down on bank lending imposed by the Government would make it very difficult for any loan request to be accommodated. Any such request would be looked at very critically and he was advised to make out the case for the loan carefully, and show quite clearly that it could be repaid within a few months.

He was now preparing for this critical meeting with the branch manager and the regional director of the bank.

Exhibit 15.1 Wendover Electronics Limited

Balance Sheet as at

	31 Dec. 1967 (Actual) £	31 Dec. 1968 (Actual) £	30 June 1969 (Estimated) £
Fixed Assets			
Plant and Machinery at Cost	67 369	75 920	75 430
Less Depreciation	39 342	44 980	47 780
	28 027	30 940	27 650
Insurance Policy (Surrender Value)	2590	3120	3650
Investment in Associated Company	1000	1000	1000
Current Assets			
Stocks: Materials	18 800	17 946	8800
Work in Progress	14 760	15 340	14 000
Debtors	58 210	67 638	76 420
Prepayments	8740	9364	7898
Cash in Hand and at Bank	1642	2981	3472
	102 152	113 269	110 590
Less *Current Liabilities*			
Bank Overdraft	24 762	19 342	102
Accounts Payable	6921	8310	9400
Accrued Liabilities	1321	1420	1086
Corporation Tax*	8124	8340	15 942
Dividend	500	500	—
	41 628	37 912	26 530
Net Working Capital	60 524	75 357	84 060
Net Assets	£92 141	£110 417	£116 360

Sources of Funds

8% Preference Shares	10 000	10 000	10 000
Ordinary Share Capital	50 000	50 000	50 000
Capital Reserve	11 215	800	—
Retained Profits	12 586	33 827	46 280
	83 801	94 627	106 280
Future Tax†	8340	15 790	10 080
	£92 141	£110 417	£116 360

*Payable on 1 January following, in a single payment.
†Payable one year after the following 1 January.

Exhibit 15.2 Wendover Electronics Limited
Profit and Loss Accounts

	Year to 31 Dec. **1967** (Actual)	Year to 31 Dec. **1968** (Actual)	6 months to 30 June **1969** (Estimated)
	£	£	£
Sales	389 180	451 200	232 370
Cost of Goods Sold			
Materials	41 260	53 780	26 444
Labour	91 734	102 460	57 696
Manufacturing Overheads (Including Depreciation)	197 423	217 605	103 973
Gross Profit	58 763	77 355	44 257
Administration and Selling Expenses	38 697	40 320	21 824
Trading Profit	20 066	37 035	22 433
Corporation Tax	8340	15 790	10 080
Profit after Tax	£11 726	£21 245	£12 353

16

Bedford Industries Limited

The planning group of Bedford Industries has been investigating a new investment project, centred around the expansion of the company's production capacity through the acquisition of a new plant which is likely to be situated on the Treforest Trading Estate in South Wales. From their investigations of the proposals that have been put forward by operating managers and their staffs, it appears that the project would require the investment of approximately £500 000. When fully established, the new plant should improve the company's profits by some £90 000 before tax and £49 500 after tax at the current rate of 45%.

Bedford Industries was started in 1918 by two armourers, William Fosdick and Albert Wright, after they had been demobilized. The company only employed two or three people until shortly before the outbreak of war in 1939. During the depression of the 'thirties, Wright gave up his interest to Fosdick and control remained in the Fosdick family hands until the company went public in 1961.

The major part of the growth of the company occurred during the Second World War, when the plant was employed almost exclusively on Ministry of Supply work: this work consisted of ammunition containers, materials handling equipment, pallets, and similar items. In view of the expertise that was thus gained in that class of work, Fosdick decided to specialize in small, light material containers which could be used in industry, and racking for use in materials stores. During the electronic revolution of the 'fifties, specialized plastic and wooden containers were developed for the handling and transportation of delicate electronic equipment.

The founder of the business had been reared in a strict Victorian household where debt was abhorred and would not be countenanced under any circumstances. This attitude he had carried into the business, and, until his death in 1952, the possibility of the company borrowing money was unthinkable; and, for a long time after his death, this prejudice continued to be an important force in managerial thinking.

His son, the present chairman and managing director, Charles Fosdick took over the reins at the age of 40. He immediately began a reconstruction of the management of the company, and set the end of 1960 as a target date for 'going public'. The company was structured into four semi-autonomous units based upon a division of the company's business by type of manufacturing process.

This reorganization took some time to effect, and its benefits did not emerge until the accounting year ended 31 December 1960, when turnover exceeded £1 300 000 and profits were just over £140 000. It was on the projection of these figures that the decision was made late in 1960 to go public during 1961.

At the time of the public issue, 44·5% of the capital was offered leaving the directors and their families owning the balance of 55·5%. Subsequently, family trusts and individual directors disposed of a further 20% of the company's shares at issue through the market, so that the shares were fairly widely held and no director held more than 10%. Part of this disposal occurred through the directors and their family trusts not taking up rights issues which had been used as the sole source of new funds during the period.

On the 18 September 1969, the board of directors met to discuss, among other things, the proposal to acquire the Treforest plant, and to decide on how the acquisition was to be financed. Mr Anthony Jones, a partner in the firm's merchant bankers, attended this meeting at the request of Mr Fosdick. Following the decision to proceed with the Treforest acquisition, Mr Jones reported to the board that, in the view of his firm, the cost of the acquisition should be financed by a debenture issue of £500 000 at 10% over a period of 20 years. He had had discussions with a number of institutional investors and he thought that they would be prepared to invest in such an issue at approximately par or with a small discount. Provision could probably be secured for the repayment of the loan to start after five years by instalments of £20 000 per year, the balance outstanding on 31 December 1990 to be repaid on that date. He explained to the board that although the rate of 10% was high it was in line with current long-term interest rates and the board should look at the after tax cost rather than the gross cost. With a tax rate on the company of

45%, the net cost of the interest charge would only be 5·5%.

Charles Fosdick's rejoinder was reminiscent of his father's. 'I'm not paying that rate of interest. Its usurious! I don't see why we should depart from our normal practice of calling on shareholders to put up the money that we need through a rights issue. If we were to issue say 500 000 new shares at 22s, this would raise enough money to cover the requirements of the Treforest acquisition and cover the issue costs. With a dividend of 20% or 1s per share, this would cost the company only just over 4·5%.'

Jim Bond, who had been the company's production manager before his retirement two years previously, added, 'As far as I can see, the cost of the debt that you are proposing is much greater than the 5·5% net that you say. How are we going to repay it? Whether it is by annual instalments as proposed or in a lump sum at the end of the 20 years, we will have to put aside money to repay the £500 000. For example, on the basis that the whole £500 000 is repaid by equal annual instalments in each of the 20 years' life of the loan (which would be the average rate at which we would have to accumulate money in any case to repay the loan) this would mean that we would have to put aside £25 000 in each year. On my reckoning, this would add another 5% to the cost.'

Joe Blake, an old friend of Fosdicks, was a little kinder to the loan proposal, 'As I see it,' he said, 'the new project will add some £90 000 pretax earnings to last year's level of £213 000, but it will only incur an interest cost of £50 000 before tax. It will therefore add £40 000 to the pretax earnings. In view of the very unexciting record of our company since it went public, this addition would considerably enhance the value of the ordinary shares.'

Philip Edgerton, the finance director, who had been silent up to this point now chipped in. 'I feel that it would not be right to sell the company's shares at 22s if we were to make a rights issue. The book value of the assets per share comes out at nearly 27s per share. If we add 500 000 new shares and £500 000 cash, this will drop to less than 25s per share, even after taking into account the new funds brought in. This would injure the interests of our existing share-holders. Nor is this the end of the story. We recently received a valuation of the company's premises made at our request by Fowler, Green & Company, and this shows that the value of the premises is currently £750 000, or some £642 000 more than the book value.'

Anthony Jones interjected at this point. 'I don't know about dilution of assets per share, but I do know that the earnings will be diluted if you proceed with a rights issue. Last year's earnings were nearly 2s 6d per share. If you add another 500 000 shares to those already issued, those earnings would have been under 1s 8d. Quite frankly, I believe that one of the reasons that the share price is not better than it is has been the effect of financing the company's expansion solely through rights issues. Not only has this diluted income, but also as shareholders have realized that they would be subjected to continuing demands for new funds they have tended to discount this factor in the share price. You all seem also to have forgotten about the effect of inflation. Under the Wilson Government, inflation in the last couple of years has been over 5%. If this was to continue, the real value of the loan repayment would not be £500 000 in 20 years' time, but something under £250 000 in real terms.'

'Yes,' interjected Fosdick, 'but what happens if President Nixon halts inflation in the States. This is bound to reflect back on conditions in this country.'

After a considerable amount of discussion, sometimes heated, Fosdick adjourned the meeting. 'It seems to me that this is much more complex than we first thought. Perhaps we had better sleep on it before we come to any conclusions.'

Exhibit 16.1 Bedford Industries Limited

Summary Balance Sheet as at 31 December 1968

Liabilities	£		Fixed Assets	£
Share Capital:			Buildings	108 200
Authorized and Issued			Machinery and Plant	
1 000 000 5s Ordinary	250 000		(net)	249 200
Capital Reserves	135 120		Other Plant (net)	71 600
Retained Profits	964 400			
	———			429 000
	1 349 520		Goodwill, Patents, etc.	91 640
Current Liabilities			*Current Assets*	
Trade Creditors	189 660		Stocks and WIP	799 200
Accrued Expenses	12 420		Debtors	324 820
Tax Due 1.1.69	111 700		Cash	18 640
	313 780			1 142 660
	£1 663 300			£1 663 300

Exhibit 16.2 Bedford Industries Limited

Five Year Financial Record

Year	Sales £	Net Profit Before Tax £	Net Profit After Tax £	Earnings Per Share	Dividends	Share Price High	Low
1964	1 632 400	158 262	†74 320	1·858s	25%	29s 6d	24s 3d
1965	1 750 090	207 621	123 200	*2·464s	20%	52s 6d	30s 9d
1966	1 398 760	74 372	43 500	·870s	20%	48s 4d	23s 3d
1967	1 682 640	116 400	65 300	1·306s	20%	33s 0d	25s 0d
1968	2 090 340	213 000	123 540	2·471s	20%	49s 6d	37s 4d
1969					‡20%	47s 8d	36s 0d

*Rights issue on 25 January 1965 of 1 for 4 at 10s.

†Profit after Profits Tax of 15% and Income Tax at 7s 9d in £. In subsequent years, at the appropriate rate of Corporation Tax.

‡Forecast rate.

17

Ambler Electronics Limited

Ambler Electronics Limited was established in 1959 by the present directors, George Ambler and Reginald Touche. Ambler had worked in the electronics industry since graduating as an electrical engineer in 1935. Initially, he had been employed by the Post Office, but during the war years had been drawn into the design and development of radar. In 1946, he used his accumulated savings to buy a small electrical manufacturing business; this he intended to use as the vehicle for marketing some new products which he thought he would be able to develop.

Shortly after he acquired this business, he began to realize that his training had not equipped him with the skills necessary to develop a successful and growing business. Prior to this, he had been solely concerned with the scientific and technical aspects of product development. Now, he realized that skills related to marketing and financial management would be required if he was to succeed. As the day to day problems of management began to absorb most of his efforts and the business began to go downhill, he decided to cut his losses by selling the business and find employment which would broaden his experience.

To this end, he joined a major electronics firm where he was concerned with the marketing and development aspects of a small team promoting new products. As such, he was not directly working on research, and continued to develop some of his ideas during his leisure hours.

By the winter of 1957 to 1958, he was satisfied that the equipment he had designed (which was in the field of microwave measuring) had reached a marketable standard. He could foresee that the product would have applications not only in measuring, but also in the future, for cooking purposes, both commercially in restaurants, etc., and in the home. During 1958, he looked around for a backer for the project and after some time was introduced to Reginald Touche.

At that time, Touche was in his early sixties. During the First World War, he had served in the Royal Engineers and, later, in the Royal Flying Corps. On demobilization, he had purchased some surplus aircraft and had built up over the years a successful business in ferrying freight and passengers for oil and other companies in the Near and Far East. The rising tide of nationalism in the areas he served had finally convinced him of the need to sell out, and in 1957 he sold the whole of his business to local interests and returned to the UK.

Touche had always retained an interest in scientific matters, and was impressed by the ideas put up to him by Ambler. He had a ready grasp of the technical problems involved in the manufacture of high precision equipment and of the need for the right marketing approach in a very specialized technical field. He was himself looking for suitable projects in which to place his capital and which would benefit from his management experience. On balance, he felt that Ambler's proposition was the best that he had considered to date, and one that would provide him with a satisfying second career and good capital appreciation on his investment.

Following their initial agreement to combine resources, the first problem was to secure adequate premises. Both men realized that it would be unwise to start with very small premises and then be faced, from time to time, with the cost and delays associated with removals, probably to areas where they would have to train new workers. On the other hand, they did not want to tie up too much of their capital in bricks and mortar.

Eventually, they were able to purchase a dilapidated warehouse of some 50 000 square feet together with some office accommodation. They did not propose to occupy the whole of this immediately, but to bring sections of it up to the required standards of cleanliness as and when required. Because of its state, they were eventually able to secure the premises for £12 500. In November 1958, the company was incorporated with a capital of £50 000 and, after the acquisition of the property, a start was made to recruit and train the required labour.

Surprisingly, the company sold £52 000 of its products in the period to 31 December 1959, and a small profit was made during that year, in spite of the cost of converting part of the premises.

Share Capital

The £50 000 capital was provided by the two partners in equal amounts. That from Touche was subscribed in cash, but half of Ambler's contribution was in the form of the development expenditures which he had incurred and the value of the patent's transferred to the business. In 1961, considerable funds were laid out in bringing the remainder of the premises up to the standard required by the business. To cover these requirements and to cover the working capital needs of the rapidly expanding business, a mortgage of £50 000 was raised on the property against a further £50 000 funds loaned by Touche. The rate of interest provided for was 9%.

In 1967, it was decided to bring the issued capital more into line with the capital employed. The building was revalued by Taylor and Blight who estimated the value at that time as being £89 000. A resolution was then approved at an extraordinary meeting of the company to increase the authorized share capital to £150 000 in £1 shares and to capitalize the capital and revenue reserves by means of a scrip issue on a two for one basis.

In preparation for the public issue and quotation for the company, the authorized capital was increased to £500 000 on the 26 September 1969 and the shares divided into 2s shares. As a result the share capital currently appears as follows:

Authorized Capital: 5 000 000 Ordinary Shares of 2s each	£500 000
Issued Capital: 1 500 000 Ordinary Shares of 2s each	£150 000

Dividends

Dividends paid during the period were kept to a minimum to conserve cash, the amounts paid being:

Year	Rate	Amount	Year	Rate	Amount
1959	nil	nil	1964	2%	£1000
1960	nil	nil	1965	10%	£5000
1961	nil	nil	1966	10%	£5000
1962	nil	nil	1967	$3\frac{1}{3}\%$	£5000
1963	2%	£1000	1968	$3\frac{1}{3}\%$	£5000

Development of Business

Over the ten years that the company has been in business, its products had developed along three different lines. The original microwave measuring and other equipment had not grown to the extent that had been hoped, although it represented just under a third of total sales value and contributed some 45% of trading profit.

The largest section of the business by sales value was the sub-contract division. This had originated in the early years when neighbouring firms who were short of capacity were glad to subcontract work. Touche had seen this as an opportunity for building up the firm's capacity, and through personal contacts had established close trading links with a number of them. This division provided some 40% of sales by value, but severe competition in recent years, plus the merger of a number of their customers, had trimmed margins.

The third product group was of more recent origin, and is founded upon computer technology. The products are printed circuits and, latterly, miniaturized circuits. Both directors feel that this may provide the best pattern of growth and profit in the next few years. Already, it provides almost 30% of sales value and profit.

Relations with the Bank

The company's bankers were the Near and Far East Bank Limited, who had been Touche's bankers for over 30 years. The growth of the business had been assisted considerably by support from this source. Touche knew the bank's directors on a personal basis and he had pursued a vigorous policy of making the company and its activities known to bank officials. This had permitted the company to enjoy generous overdraft facilities.

In August 1969, the bank manager wrote to the company about a number of outstanding affairs. Included in that letter was the following:

As a result of Government directives to the banks to reduce overall lending to within limits laid down by the Treasury, we are reluctantly forced to reconsider all overdraft limits. As you know, your own arrangements are due for review in October, and we would wish to give you as advanced notice as possible about the bank's position when this is discussed. Unless there is any drastic change in Government policy in the meantime, we regret that we will not be able to increase in any way the current level of £200 000. You will appreciate that in the past we have been able to meet your requirements in line with your increasing activities. This year this will not be possible.

We must also draw your attention to the current overdraft

position. This is some £47 000 above the agreed limit and we would ask you to pull down the amount overdrawn to within the £200 000 limit as soon as possible.

The agreed interest rate on the overdraft facilities was $1\frac{1}{2}\%$ above bank rate, which at that time stood at 8%.

The Public Issue

As a result of the bank's letter a series of discussions took place with the company's financial advisers, Arbor, Mills, Joclyn & Company. It was decided, as a matter of urgency, to explore the possibility of a public issue and, at the same time, obtaining a stock exchange quotation for the company.

A number of factors contributed to this decision. Because of his advancing age, Touche wished to reduce his interest in the business so that he could pursue arrangements that he had in hand to reduce death duties. Although the close company provisions had not been an unduly onerous burden on the company, because its need to retain profits was evident at all times, it was considered desirable to escape any further disability by becoming a non-close company.

Ambler also took the view that this would be an opportune time to sell some of his shares, so that he could enjoy those fruits of his labours that only a capital sum could provide. He was not keen, however, that his shareholding should fall below 35% of the total shares at issue.

In view of the bank's continuing support, it was felt that the provision of £150 000 new funds would provide adequate working capital for the next few years. This would be raised by an issue of new shares. Based upon the 1968 balance sheet values, this would put a book value on the equity of £407 300.

Forecast of Profits

The directors estimate that the profit for the current year will amount to £50 000 before tax, but that there is every prospect of it reaching £60 000 for the following year.

Pricing the Issue

Currently under discussion is the price at which the shares will be offered to the public. A preliminary assessment of the effect of a number of issue prices has been made as follows:

Issue price	Number of new shares to be issued	Total issued shares	Price earnings ratio
4s	750 000	2 250 000	9
6s	500 000	2 000 000	12
8s	375 000	1 875 000	15
10s	300 000	1 800 000	18

On the basis that Touche disposed of 50% of his holding and Ambler 10%, then, with a P/E ratio of 15, the shares would be held in the following proportions:

Touche	375 000 shares	20%
Ambler	675 000 shares	36%
Public	825 000 shares	44%
	1 875 000 shares	100%

Comparative Issues

During the discussions as to the price at which the shares are to be offered, data relating to other issues as shown in Exhibit 17.3 were considered.

Staff

In addition to Ambler and Touche, the company secretary also had a seat on the board. He had been with Touche in his old firm, and had managed the financial affairs of the company since its inception. He was now approaching his sixty-third birthday. The remaining senior management are shown in Exhibit 17.4.

Stock Market Indices

The *Financial Times* actuaries shares indices gave the following information relating to the electrical and electronic industries:

	Number of Companies in sample	P/E ratio	Dividend yield
Electricals (Excl. Light Electricals and Electronics)	(11)	16·18	3·56
Electricals (Light Electronic and Radio)	(15)	19·28	2·88

Exhibit 17.1 Ambler Electronics Limited

Balance Sheet as at 31 December 1968

USES		£ 000s	
	Cost	Depreciation	
Fixed Assets			
Land and Buildings (as revalued 1967)	89·0	—	89·0
Plant and Equipment	143·1	89·5	53·6
Tools	6·3	3·2	3·1
Vehicles	3·4	1·9	1·5
	241·8	94·6	147·2

Patents, etc.   3·3

Current Assets		
Stocks and Work in Progress		334·8
Debtors		371·8
Prepayments		6·3
Cash		3·4
		716·3
Less *Current Liabilities*		
Bank Overdraft	247·3	
Trade Creditors	227·4	
Accruals	5.1	
Tax due 1.1.69	26·7	
Dividends	5·0	
		511·5

Net Current Assets   204·8

Net Assets   £355·3

SOURCES
Owner's Funds:
Authorized Capital 5 000 000 2s Ordinary Shares   500·0

Issued Capital 1 500 000 2s Ordinary Shares   150·0
Capital Reserve   25·1
Retained Profits   82·2

                                                                                   257·3
Future Tax (payable 1.1.70)   48·0
9% *Mortgage* (Charged on Land and Buildings)   50·0

                                                                                   £355·3

Exhibit 17.2 Ambler Electronics Limited

Ten Year Record of Profits

Year	Sales	Operating expenses (excl. deprn.)	Deprecia-tion	Trading profit	Other income	Interest payable	Directors fees, etc.	Net profit	Tax	Profits after tax
1959	52 000	44 000	2000	6000	—	—	5000	1000	—	1000
1960	76 000	63 000	3000	10 000	—	—	7500	2500	500	2000
1961	221 000	221 000	5000	(5000)	2000	4500	7500	(15 000)	—	(15 000)
1962	442 000	396 000	7000	39 000	2000	4500	7500	29 000	5000	24 000
1963	523 000	475 000	8000	40 000	3000	4500	9000	29 500	14 000	15 500
1964	347 000	313 000	12 000	22 000	2000	4500	8000	11 500	4000	7500
1965	592 000	525 000	13 000	54 000	2000	4500	15 000	36 500	17 000	19 500
1966	874 000	798 000	15 000	61 000	2000	4500	16 000	42 500	20 000	22 500
1967	1 372 000	1 277 000	17 000	78 000	2000	4500	17 500	58 000	27 000	31 000
1968	1 943 000	1 805 000	23 000	115 000	2000	4500	17 500	95 000	48 000	47 000

Exhibit 17.3 Ambler Electronics Limited

Comparative Issues

Company	Type of business	Date made public	Issued capital	1969 price range	Current price	Dividend %	Times divi. covered	Gross yield %	Price/earnings
Painton	Development, design and manufacture of electronic components	1962	600 000 ordinary shares of 5s	67s 0d to 32s 6d	66s 3d	23½	2·7	1·8	20·7
Louis Newmark	Electronic and mechanical instrument manufacturer	1961	£741 151 Ordinary in shares of 5s £250 000 8% Pref. £300 000 7½% Pref.	30s 0d to 18s 0d	20s 0d	13·9	3·0	3·4	9·6
Electronic Machine	Manufacturer of electronic industrial equipment	1947	£551 520 in ordinary 5s shares	25s 3d to 17s 0d	18s 3d	10	2·9	2·7	12·6
Carbon Electric Holdings	Manufacturer of data processing and logging equipment, components, thermocouple systems, film wire circuitry for electronics industry, carbon products	1961	£275 000 in ordinary shares of 1s each	8s 3d to 4s 0d	6s 0d	12½	3·0	2·1	15·6

Exhibit 17.4 Ambler Electronics Limited : Organizational Structure

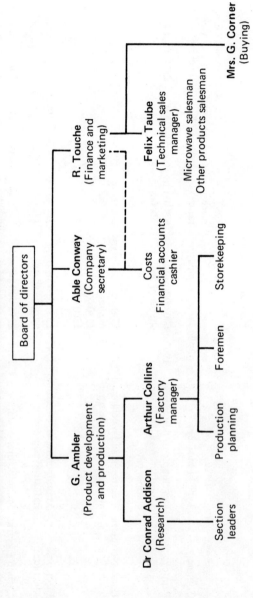

18

Wilkinson Warburton Limited

'Well, I think that that is about as far as we can go at the moment Sir George,' concluded Michael Rosenberg. 'As soon as we are a little nearer the issue date, we will make a final decision about the price.'

Michael Rosenberg was a member of the merchant banking firm of Samuel Montague & Company Limited, who were to handle the floatation of Wilkinson Warburton Limited on the London Stock Exchange by means of an offer for sale of some of the ordinary shares.

The Company

The business was started in 1834 by one John Wilkinson of Halifax, and traded as wholesale furnishers and general textile warehousemen. The present chairman of the group, Sir George Martin, KBE, LLD, became a partner in 1915, and in 1925 the business was incorporated as a private limited company and Sir George was joined by the present deputy chairman, Frank Marshall, MBE. For many years, the company traded from small premises in Leeds followed by large city centre premises.

As a result of a study of wholesaling in the USA, it was decided to move from the congested city centre to new premises where there would be adequate parking, delivery, and dispatch facilities. Such premises were found in 1966 at Pudsey in Yorkshire. The location offered easy access to all parts of the Midlands and North of England, particularly with the opening of the M1 motorway (London–Leeds) and the Leeds–Manchester motorway.

When the reconstruction of the new premises was completed, they comprised specially designed warehouses to carry women's and children's wear, men's and boy's clothing, bedding, furnishing, and other items, covering the whole range of textile goods with good display and viewing facilities, together with a modern restaurant, large goods inwards and dispatch docks, and a car park for 500 cars.

A purpose built carpet warehouse of 35 000 square feet was completed in 1969; this enables the company to carry 2000 rolls of Broadloom, making it one of the largest wholesale suppliers of carpets in the UK.

In 1966, the company acquired Crowe and Company Limited, an old established business in the same field, and the latter's activities were transferred to the new premises. At the time that the issue was under consideration, the company was served by 60 full-time sales representatives, who primarily covered the North of England. All sales are to the retail trade, mostly under the firm's registered trademark Caressa. As an essential part of its overall selling policy, the company considers it necessary to extend credit to its retail customers.

The merchandize that the company offers to its customers is garnered from all over the world by 23 full-time buyers.

Profit Record and Prospects

The combined profits of the group before tax for the 10 years to 19 July 1969, subject to the notes below, were as follows:

Year end 19 July	Turnover £	Depreciation £	Profits less losses before taxation £
1960	1 946 167	9601	87 133
1961	2 261 521	9872	97 899
1962	2 459 187	11 146	108 062
1963	2 534 629	14 961	104 582
1964	2 901 121	13 505	137 566
1965	3 060 161	12 809	146 778
1966	3 062 720	13 675	122 590
1967	4 429 797	31 062	111 271
1968	4 431 744	31 695	199 105
1969	4 578 678	34 910	233 332

Notes

1. The amounts shown as profits are before charging tax, but after all expenses, including depreciation and directors' remuneration.
2. No depreciation is provided on freehold land and buildings; the annual charges for depreciation of fixtures, fittings, and equipment, and motor vehicles, have been recalculated for the eight years to the 19 July 1967, to put them on the same basis as those operated since that date, e.g.:

	Rates on reducing balance
Fixtures, Fittings, and Equipment	15%
Motor Vehicles	25%

The drop in profits for the year to 19 July 1967 were due to the expenses in connection with the move into new premises, together with those incurred by the merger with Crowe and Company Limited.

The profits for the first six months of the current year, i.e., the period to 19 January 1970, are higher than those for the same period in the previous year, and the directors estimate that, in the absence of unforeseen circumstances, profits before tax for the whole year should not be less than £250 000. On this basis, there would be £126 808 available for the ordinary shareholders, viz.:

	£
Estimated Profits before Taxation	250 000
Less Corporation Tax at 45%	112 500
	137 500
Preference Dividends	10 692
Available to Ordinary Shareholders	£126 808

Capital Changes

On the 17 February 1970, the authorized and issued capital of the company was made up as follows:

	Authorized £	Issued £
6% Redeemable Cumulative Preference Shares of £1	100 000	90 711
7% Non-Cumulative Second Preference Shares of £1	75 000	75 000
Ordinary Shares of £1 each	150 000	150 000

On the 18 February 1970, the ordinary shares were divided into ordinary shares of 5s each, and, at the same time, the authorized share capital was increased to £775 000 by the creation of a further 1 800 000 ordinary shares of 5s of which 1 400 000 were issued, credited as fully paid, by way of capitalization of reserves.

Dividends

Dividends paid on the company's shares over the last five years were as follows:

Year to 19 July	6% Redeemable Cumulative preference	7% Non-Cumulative second preference	Ordinary shares
1965	6%	7%	7%
1966	6%	7%	7%
1967	6%	7%	7%
1968	6%	7%	7%
1969	6%	7%	7%
1970 Half Year	3%	3½%	2½% Interim

It would be the directors' intention, subsequent to the public issue, to pay a final dividend for the current year of 10% on the capital then issued and, in following years, subject to the level of profits being similar to those for the current year, to pay approximately 70% of available earnings as dividends. On this basis, the dividend for the following year would be 18% covered 1·4 times.

The Shares to be Offered

The proposals that have been discussed by the board with its financial advisers are that 865 000 of the ordinary shares presently owned by various shareholders will be acquired by Samuel Montague & Company Limited, and offered for sale to the public at a price yet to be fixed.

Following such an issue, the directors and their families would be beneficially interested in 552 118 ordinary shares, or approximately 27·6% of the issued ordinary shares. In addition, there are interests in a further 517 160 ordinary shares.

Management and Staff

The group employs some 400 people in all. Sir George Martin and Mr Frank Marshall, who have presided over the growth of the company for a period of over 35 years, are now aged 85 and 70 years respectively. The other senior staff include Mr P. J. D. Marshall, son of Mr Frank Marshall, who is 36 years of age and, as well as acting as joint managing director with his father, specializes in the merchandizing side of the business; Mr Arthur Britton, aged 56, who has been with the company since 1928, acts as director and company secretary; Mr Alan H. Crowe, aged 59, who joined the board in 1966 following the acquisition of his company, is responsible for credit control; Mr K. C. Bradley, aged 29, who is the sales manager; and Mr D. Thrippleton, aged 38, who acts as personnel and general manager.

Sir George proposes to step down from office as chairman after the first annual general meeting of the company after the issue; he will be succeeded by Frank Marshall. Other executive directors have entered into service agreements with the company for periods of five years.

Special Provisions of the Articles of Association

The articles of association provide *inter alia* that the company shall be at liberty, at any time on or after 31 March 1967, to redeem all or any of the redeemable preference shares at par plus a premium of 2s 6d per share, upon giving the registered holders not less than six months' notice in writing of its intention to do so.

The ability of the directors to borrow monies is restricted to a sum equal to one and one-half times the adjusted capital and reserves of the company and its subsidiaries.

Other Information

The *Financial Times* for the 24 February showed in the FTA indices, the following information for the textile group which is based upon the results of 24 companies:

Estimated Earnings Yield	6·96%
Estimated Dividend Yield	5·18%
Estimated Price Earnings Ratio	14·37

The balance sheet for the company as at 19 July 1969, as adjusted for such changes as were thought appropriate by the reporting accountants, is shown in Exhibit 18.1.

Data relating to a number of companies in the industry are shown in Exhibit 18.2.

The group has received clearances in respect of liability to surtax under section 245 of the Income Tax Act, 1952, for all relevant periods up to 5 April 1966, and in respect of shortfall assessments under section 77 of the Finance Act, 1965, for the periods from 6 April 1966 to 19 July 1969. Under the agreements with the vendors of the shares, they have provided indemnities against the consequences of liabilities to estate duty, income tax, surtax, and to the special charge.

Exhibit 18.1 Wilkinson Warburton Limited

Balance Sheet as at 19 July 1969

	Cost or valuation £	Depreciation £	£
Fixed Assets			
Freehold Land and Buildings at Valuation	447 250	—	447 250
Freehold Land and Buildings at Cost	6036	—	6036
Fixtures, Fittings, and Equipment	161 164	69 374	91 790
Motor Vehicles	99 736	24 911	74 825
	714 186	94 285	619 901

Trademarks—at cost less amounts written off	1
Trade Investments	2723

Current Assets		
Stock—at lower of cost and net realizable value	536 216	
Debtors and Prepayments	699 785	
Cash in Hand	618	
	1 236 619	

Less *Current Liabilities*		
Creditors and Accrued Charges	121 209	
Current Taxation	77 706	
Bank Overdraft	180 085	
Proposed Dividend (Gross)	12 096	
	391 096	

Net Current Assets	845 523
	1 468 148

Deduct		
Corporation Tax payable 1 January 1971	105 000	
Tax Equalization Account*	18 500	
	123 500	

Net Tangible Assets	£1 344 648

*The tax equalization account represents corporation tax at 45% on the excess of book values, of fixtures, fittings, equipment, and motor vehicles, at 19 February 1969, over the written down values for tax purposes.

Exhibit 18.2 Wilkinson Warburton Limited
Financial Data of Companies in the Industry

	Blackwood Morton & Sons (Holdings)	Carrington & Dewhurst	Aquascutum	Cook & Watts	William Pickles	Wardle Bernard	Bury & Masco
Equity capital (£ ms)	2·0	14·53	0·9	1·64	1·53	0·90	1·62
Assets per share	13s 10d	9s 0d	3s 3d	8s 5d	3s 6d	3s 1d	10s 5d
Nominal share value	5s 0d	5s 0d	1s 0d	5s 0d	2s 0d	1s 0d	5s 0d
Earnings per share (%):							
1964	35·2	18·0	53·6	14·6	18·3	68·5	31·2
1965	29·7	39·9	35·9	8·5	15·6	56·0	26·4
1966	23·2	28·7	33·6	7·0	14·3	55·5	21·6
1967	13·6	15·5	37·8	4·3	14·9	54·4	22·9
1968	37·6	15·2	40·0	6·0	13·3	57·0	21·9
1969	29·9	22·2	—	—	—	29·6 (forecast)	—
Dividends (%):							
1964	17·5	12·5	25·0	8·0	8·6	30·0	20·0‡
1965	17·5	17·5	27·5	8·0	9·4	30·0	20·0†
1966	17·5	20·0	27·5	8·0	9·4	30·0	20·0
1967	12·5	15·0	27·5	5·0	9·4	32·5	20·0
1968	17·5	15·0	28·0	6·0	9·8	33·64	20·0
1969	17·5	16·0*	28·0	*	—	—	—

(continued overleaf)

Exhibit 18.2 (continued)

Average share price:

1964	11s 3d	13s 6d	5s 7d	6s 2d	2s 9d	7s 3d	12s 7d
1965	10s 10d	16s 1d	5s 11d	6s 4d	2s 2d	6s 0d	11s 7d
1966	9s 7d	16s 0d	5s 9d	6s 2d	2s 11d	5s 2d	12s 10d
1967	8s 0d	13s 1d	5s 10d	6s 7d	2s 3d	5s 9d	12s 4d
1968	12s 0d	18s 6d	7s 4d	5s 5d	2s 9d	7s 5d	14s 1d
Share price 23 Feb 1970	10s 9d	9s 8¾d	6s 9d	3s 6d	2s 9¾d	3s 3¾d	7s 4½d
Latest dividend	17·5%	*	28%	*	10%	20%	20%
Times covered	1·7	*	1·3	*	1·4	—	1·1
Gross dividend yield	8·1%	*	4·1%	*	7·1%	6·0%	13·6%
Price earnings ratio	7·3	*	18·8	*	10·4	—	7·0
Principal activities	Manufacturer of carpets, felts, etc.	Weaving, finishing and merchanting of manmade fibre, cloths	Clothing manufacturer, wholesaler and retailer	Textile warehousemen, wholesalers and manufacturers	Manufacturers, merchants, and exporters of cotton and rayon goods	Fabrics, furnishings, plastics, and leathercloth	Felt carpet manufacturers

*Dividend since reduced.
‡Also 3⅓% capital distribution.
†Also 1·25% capital distribution.

94

19

GW Construction Company Limited

Mr Gerald Wentworth has been deeply concerned about the future of the above company of which he is chairman and managing director. Having operated for a number of years as a private, family company, he is now acutely aware of the penalties imposed upon close companies by the 1965 Finance Act, and of the desirability of strengthening the management of the company to ensure adequate profitability in the future. These factors have turned his mind for some time towards the desirability of obtaining a public quotation on a stock exchange for the company.

Wentworth is 56 years old and inherited the company from his father who died in 1946. At that time, he had just been demobilized after serving in the armed forces during the Second World War. The business had been started in 1896 by Wentworth's great-grandfather in a London suburb and had been mainly engaged in the repair and maintenance work on houses and small shops; occasionally, a complete house was built to customers' specification.

The business has shown no growth up to 1939. At the outbreak of war it employed, in addition to Gerald Wentworth and his father, two craftsmen on a permanent basis. Shortly after the declaration of war, Wentworth and his two craftsmen joined HM Forces leaving his father to 'nurse' the business during the war years.

Wentworth joined the Royal Engineers in late 1940, and during his service with them he gained experience in a number of fields related to building and construction work, and as time went on he began to study the implications of controlling projects involving more than two or three men. Towards the end of the war, he began to think about ways in which this experience could be of use in the family business to which he would be returning, and he began to formulate plans for its expansion which he hoped his father would accept when he was released from the forces.

On returning to civilian life, Wentworth found his father in ill health and, on his death, in September 1946 he found himself in sole control of the business. It was extremely run-down, and this, together with a scarcity of skilled labour in the area, meant that more ambitious projects had to be shelved; work was mainly concentrated upon war damage repairs and general maintenance work. During this period, the profits of the business were largely ploughed back to provide a more stable financial base. At the same time, he endeavoured to gather around him a team of people whom he felt had some potential should he be able to expand the business in the way that he desired. When private house-building became more liberalized in the 'fifties, he began to establish a business based upon it, using the profits so made to acquire small sites which he could develop for residential purposes.

The business had progressed slowly at first, but, in the late 'fifties, had grown at a much faster rate, and to the original business of house-building he had added shops, offices, and, latterly, factory buildings. He had been assisted in this process by his two sons, John and Peter, aged 29 and 27 respectively, who had joined him in the business.

Incorporation of the Business

The growth in the size of the organization had led Wentworth to incorporate the business in January 1960 as a private company. The company acquired the business from him for £82 660, which was satisfied by the issue to him of £50 000 £1 ordinary shares in GW Construction Company Limited, the balance of the purchase consideration being left as a loan to the company, to be repaid over the next three years. In view of the increasing participation in the business by his sons, and with a view as to the possible effects of estate duty should he die, the shares issued by the company had been distributed among his family in the following way:

Mr G. Wentworth	25 001
Mrs G. Wentworth	2999
Mr J. Wentworth	7500
Mr P Wentworth	7500
Trust for infant daughters	7000
	50 000

On 31 March 1963, the company had approached AR Insurance Company Limited with a view to borrowing a sum of money to finance the company's continued growth. As a result of the negotiations, the insurance company loaned to GW the sum of £150 000 on an 8% mortgage debenture 1981. The security for the debenture was the freehold land and buildings owned by the company, the whole of the amount borrowed being repayable on the 31 December 1981. Interest was payable at half-yearly intervals on the 30 June and 31 December in each year. As a part of the agreement, Mr Wentworth undertook that no dividends would be paid by the company until the value of the net assets was three times the amount of the loan.

The shareholders passed a resolution on the 31 October 1965 increasing the authorized capital of the company to £125 000. At the same time, they approved a bonus issue of three new shares for every two already held, the subscription price for the bonus shares being met by a transfer from retained profits. At 31 December 1965, the balance sheet of the company was as shown in Exhibit 19.1, and the profit and loss account for the year to that date as shown in Exhibit 19.2. Wentworth estimated that the profit before tax for 1966 would be £75 000, and could see no immediate prospect of increasing that figure.

Coxley Building Company Limited

In the locality within which GWC operated, it was in competition with, among others, a company which latterly had not been very profitable due to the declining health of its owner. Mr Wentworth was well acquainted with the owner of this business, Mr F. G. Armstrong, and when the latter indicated that his health would necessitate him giving up business and retiring abroad to a warmer climate, Mr Wentworth considered the possibility of acquiring this company. It had been incorporated in 1935 under the name of Coxley Building Company Limited (CBC) and owned valuable freeholds in the area. In 1961 and 1962, it had earned profits before tax of about £40 000 per year, but this had declined due to poor management by the owner to the present level of about £25 000 per year. The balance sheet and profit and loss account for CBC for the year to 30 November 1965 are shown in Exhibits 19.3 and 19.4.

The item for freehold land and buildings shown in the balance sheet for CBC at £50 000 is considerably undervalued, and it is estimated that the current value of the properties is £128 000. The plant and machinery is in reasonable working condition, but would not be worth more than the net value as shown in the balance sheet. With proper management, Mr Wentworth considers that he could improve the profit for CBC over the next four years to double the figure for the year to 30 November 1965.

After a series of discussions between Wentworth and Armstrong and their advisers, it was agreed at a meeting on 30 June 1966 that GW Construction would have a thirty day option to purchase the whole of the issued share capital of Coxley from Armstrong for the sum of £150 000. The major difficulty in the negotiations was Armstrong's insistence that, as he was leaving the UK, the purchase price should be settled in cash rather than by shares in the enlarged GWC.

Funding the Purchase Price

The problem was, therefore, how to find the £150 000 purchase price for CBC. The question of obtaining a stock exchange quotation was raised, as it was felt that the enlarged company would be of sufficient size to warrant a quotation. Mr Wentworth was somewhat hesitant about this: he recognized that there might be some tax advantages in selling off the appropriate proportion of the equity of the company, but this would itself bring in some additional problems. His company would be brought much more directly under public scrutiny and he would have to justify his policies to what he considered to be 'outsiders'. Moreover, although the sale of shares to the public might relieve some of the worst features of the close company legislation, he was concerned with the effect that the enlargement of the equity might have on the existing shareholders.

After some discussion the following three proposals were considered to be the possible alternative ways of financing the acquisition of CBC:

1. The sale of 67 000 £1 ordinary shares in GWC to the public at 50s each. These shares would be in addition to those already issued. This would raise £167 500 which would provide the required £150 000 for the acquisition of CBC, and provide £17 500 to cover the costs of the issue and if thought desirable, obtaining a quotation.
2. The XL Finance Company Limited is prepared to lend the company the sum of £130 000 on a second mortgage debenture. The

terms for this debenture would be an interest rate of 9% and the right to subscribe for 10 000 ordinary shares in GWC at a price of 40s per share. This would give the finance company a 7·2% stake in the equity. The whole of the principal would be repayable on 31 December 1980.

3. The AR Insurance Company Limited is prepared to lend a further £150 000 to the company subject to amendment of the terms of the debenture deed. These amendments would provide for the interest rate for the whole amount borrowed to be raised to 8½%. The principal sum would be repaid by payments of £12 500 in December of each year, such repayments to commence on 31 December 1968. The balance outstanding at 31 December 1981 to be repaid on that date. The provision restricting the payment of dividends would be lifted to the extent that the rate of dividend was governed by the avoidance of a 'shortfall' assessment because the company had paid no dividend. The net amount of such dividends must be covered by directors loans back to the company.

The board of directors of GWC considered that the continuance of the business would necessitate the investment in new plant and machinery each year of sums at least equal to the amount provided for depreciation. Due to the effects of inflation, this sum might have to be supplemented out of after tax profits to provide for the higher cost of plant that is purchased. During the current series of discussions with both AR Insurance and the XL Finance, they had indicated that they were concerned with the impact that the purchase of machinery on hire purchase might have upon their security, and thought that it was likely that, in the terms of any loan that might be made as a result of the current negotiations, they would have to insert a clause severely restricting the right of the company to use this form of finance.

Information re GW Construction Company Limited

The item of Directors' Loans £125 000 shown in Exhibit 19.1 represents money obtained by the directors from private sources and the balance of the purchase price of the business, which had not, in fact, ever been paid to the vendor. On 30 June 1962, the company had issued an undertaking to repay the amount outstanding as to £20 000 by the 31 December 1968, £45 000 during the year 1969, and the balance outstanding by the 31 December 1970.

For the year 1960, GWC paid a dividend of 10% on the ordinary shares; in 1961 15%, and in 1962 15%. No dividends have been paid since, in conformity with the requirements of the mortgage debenture. CBC has paid the following dividends on its ordinary shares:

Year to 30 November 1960	25%
Year to 30 November 1961	30%
Year to 30 November 1962	30%
Year to 30 November 1963	20%
Year to 30 November 1964	10%
Year to 30 November 1965	10%

Mr A. W. Orton, the company secretary of GWC, who has been concerned with the directors in formulating the present proposals, has been examining the present commitments of the company as regards the payment of interest and the repayment of the sums borrowed. The results of his examination are shown in Exhibit 19.5. In his recent conversations with Mr Wentworth, he had been expressing his concern as to the ability of the expanded company to meet any additional borrowing to support the purchase. As he said, 'I like to sleep at night and not worry where the next £100 is to come from.'

While Mr Wentworth was aware that the raising of additional loans would put some strain upon the company, he was not happy at the dilution effect that the issue of additional ordinary shares would have upon the existing shareholders.

Exhibit 19.1 GW Construction Company Limited
Balance Sheet as at 31 December 1965

	£	£
Fixed Assets		
Freehold Land and Buildings at Cost		175 000
Plant and Machinery at Cost	221 170	
Less Depreciation	119 610	101 560
Vehicles and Mobile Plant at Cost	113 250	
Less Depreciation	69 780	
		43 470
		320 030

GW Construction Company Limited

Current Assets	£	£
Stores	176 210	
Work in Progress Less Payments Advanced	814 940	
Debtors and Prepayments	145 830	
Cash in Hand	3490	
		1 140 470
		1 460 500
Less *Current Liabilities*		
Bank Overdraft—Unsecured	141 310	
Creditors	698 260	
Accrued Liabilities	33 290	
Hire Purchase Payments Outstanding	122 410	
Loans from Directors	125 000	
Taxation Payable 1 January 1966	5382	
		1 125 652
Net Assets		£334 848

Financed as follows:		
Authorized and Issued Share Capital		
125 000 £1 Ordinary Shares		125 000
Retained Profits		29 902
		154 902
Tax Payable 1 January 1967		29 946
8% Mortgage Debenture 1981		150 000
		£334 848

Exhibit 19.2 GW Construction Company Limited

Summary Profit and Loss Account for the Year to 31 December 1965

Sales		1 691 170
Materials, Labour, Subcontract, Site Overheads		1 530 750
		160 420
General Administrative Expenses	23 127	
Depreciation of Plant, Machinery, and Vehicles	50 428	
		73 555
		86 865
Mortgage Debenture Interest		12 000
		74 865
Corporation Tax at 40%		29 946
Net Profit after Tax		£44 919

Exhibit 19.3 Coxley Building Company Limited
Balance Sheet as at 30 November 1965

	£	£
Fixed Assets		
Freehold Land and Buildings as Revalued 1938 and Subsequent Additions at Cost		50 000
Plant, Machinery, and Vehicles at Cost	73 480	
Less Depreciation	51 810	
		21 670
		71 670
Current Assets		
Stores and Work Done, but not Invoiced	249 810	
Debtors	59 540	
Prepayments	4380	
Cash in Hand and at Bank	12 360	
		326 090
		397 760
Less *Current Liabilities*		
Creditors	247 830	
Accrued Liabilities	11 370	
Taxation Payable 1 January 1966	12 820	
		272 020
Net Assets		£125 740
Financed as follows:		
Authorized Share Capital	75 000	
Issued Share Capital:		
50 000 £1 Ordinary Shares	50 000	
10 000 £1 6% Preference Shares	10 000	
		60 000
Capital Reserve		15 000
Retained Profit		41 656
		116 656
Tax Payable 1 January 1967		9084
		£125 740

Exhibit 19.4 Coxley Building Company Limited
Summary Profit and Loss Account for the Year to 30 November 1965

	£
Sales	436 210
Contract Costs	390 740
	45 470
General Administrative Expenses	20 260
Trading Profit before Tax	25 210
Corporation Tax at 40%	9084
Profit after Tax	16 126

6% Preference Dividend:	Gross	600	
	Less Tax Retained	247	
			353

Profit Available to Ordinary Shareholders	£15 773

Exhibit 19.5 GW Construction Company Limited
Schedule of Existing Debt Service Requirements

		8% Mortgage Debenture				Total
	Hire					after
	purchase	Interest	Interest		Directors'	tax
Year	repayments	before tax	after tax	Principal	loans	outlay
	£	£	£	£	£	£
1966	44 220	12 000	7200	—	—	51 420
1967	41 090	12 000	7200	—	—	48 290
1968	37 100	12 000	7200	—	20 000	64 300
1969	—	12 000	7200	—	45 000	52 200
1970	—	12 000	7200	—	60 000	67 200
1971	—	12 000	7200	—	—	7200
1972	—	12 000	7200	—	—	7200
1973	—	12 000	7200	—	—	7200
1974	—	12 000	7200	—	—	7200
1975	—	12 000	7200	—	—	7200
1976	—	12 000	7200	—	—	7200
1977		12 000	7200	—	—	7200
1978	—	12 000	7200	—	—	7200
1979	—	12 000	7200	—	—	7200
1980	—	12 000	7200	—	—	7200
1981	—	12 000	7200	150 000	—	157 200
	122 410	192 000	115 200	150 000	125 000	512 610

20

Thompsons (Contractors) Limited

Thompsons (Contractors) Limited is the result of the amalgamation of two smaller companies some five years back. The original company of that name was formed in the 'thirties by the present chairman's father. Since the Second World War, it has been mainly engaged in building factories, shops, and, to a certain extent, developing housing estates for local authorities. Built up as a small family concern between the wars, it was rapidly expanded when the chairman and managing director, Mr J. W. Thompson, rejoined the firm at the end of the war. He was then 33 years old, and, although without any qualifications, had developed an ability to nose out likely sources of contracts and to go in at the right price.

Thompson had been considering the future of his business at the stage of growth it had reached at that time when, in 1953, he met an old friend whom he had not seen for some ten years, Mr A. C. Carless. Mr Carless had been trained as an architect, and was currently collaborating with a firm which undertook similar types of work in the Midlands and traded under the name of Unibuild. The owner of the business was of advanced age, and after some twelve months' discussions Thompsons and Unibuild were merged under the present name.

The major objective of the merger was to establish a company of sufficient size ultimately to obtain a quotation on the Stock Exchange. On the 4 March 1963, the company offered for sale 30% of the shares in a public offer at a price of 22s per share. The prospectus contained the following information:

Earnings Record

Year to 31 December

Profit after Depreciation, Directors' Remuneration, etc., but before tax (£ 000s)

Year	Profit
1953	72
1954	89
1955	44
1956	32
1957	68
1958	135
1959	210
1960	162
1961	188
1962	240

Future of the Business

... The company is at present engaged in expanding its construction of industrial buildings, and expects to become more specialized in this field in the future. At the same time, the board recognize that to ensure continuity of work it may be necessary to erect factories for sale or letting on a speculative basis.

The shares were sold on the basis of an 8% dividend for the year 1963 covered 2·04 times. The relevant forecast of profits was as follows:

	£
Profit before tax	240 000
Estimated Taxation (Profits Tax and Income Tax)	130 000
	110 000
Cost of Net Dividend	53 900
	£56 100

At the offer price of 22s, an 8% dividend would provide a dividend yield of approximately 7¼%. After the issue, the 1 100 000 ordinary shares were held as follows:

Mr A. C. Carless, Technical Director	150 000
Mr F. Woolton, Director	40 000
Mr J. W. Thompson, Chairman and Managing Director	376 200
Mr F. W. Thompson, Director	77 000
Mr J. L. Thompson, Director	77 000
Mrs E. Thompson, Secretary	24 000
Associates of Mr Thompson	25 800
Public	330 000
Total	1 100 000

105

Over the years following the public issue, the level of activity expanded by almost 50%, the profit figures and share prices for the period being as follows:

Year	Profit before interest and tax £	Interest £	Profit before tax £	Highest share price for year
1963	246 000	20 000	226 000	48s 1d
1964	250 000	20 000	230 000	54s 3d
1965	194 000	20 000	174 000	26s 8d
1966	136 000	20 000	116 000	15s 9d
1967	341 000	20 000	321 000	59s 6d

The company suffered the usual setbacks due to changes in the level of activity in the home economy. From a peak turnover of £3·8 million in 1964, the value of contracts declined to £2·31 million in 1966. In an effort to maintain the level of work done, gross margins were pared to the minimum and on average dropped to around 8% of contract prices by the middle of 1966. Because of the need to devote more effort to tendering, it was found to be impossible to reduce the level of head office expenses by more than 10%. This difficulty was accentuated by the policy of the board of directors to maintain a highly competent technical staff.

Not only were the directors concerned with the quality of the staff that they employed, but also, in a drive to cut costs on contracts, laid down a policy of making the maximum use of mechanical aids. Each year the expenditure on new plant and machinery and vehicles has exceeded the depreciation charge by some £50 000.

Early in 1968, the board of directors held a weekend meeting with some of their senior staff for the purpose of discussing the future of the business. The board foresaw continuing economic difficulties, and decided that vigorous action should be taken both to consolidate the earnings level of 1967 and to lay the foundation for an advance in profits for the future. At this meeting, a survey was presented which had been commissioned some months earlier, of the likely pattern of demand for factory units in the company's area of operations. This revealed the possibility of a continuing demand for relatively simple factory units which could be built up of basic modules. At the conclusion of the meeting, the board commissioned a group of senior executives to recommend a course of action based on the following resolutions:

1. To obtain a major part of the market, costs must be reduced by the mechanization of as much as possible of the construction work so that prefabrication can be undertaken off the site.
2. To provide for continuity of work, both for construction workers and the manufacture of prefabricated sections, the company should consider the possibility of developing small trading estates on its own account and the letting unsold properties, this activity to be phased into otherwise slack periods.

On the 15 July 1968, the working group submitted its report to the main board. Among the points set out were the following:

1. The new factory units should be offered to clients as a package deal.
2. On the forecast of available work, the group felt that the new activity could add a third to the 1967 turnover. About ¼ of this increase would mature in each of the next four years.
3. The design work on the new units and the initial marketing costs are expected to amount to £200 000.
4. The purchase of suitable premises and the necessary plant and equipment to manufacture the prefabricated units is expected to cost some £250 000.
5. Provision should be made for the cost of financing units which will be retained for letting. The likely foreseeable pattern of investment would be:

1969	£30 000
1970	£50 000
1971	£80 000
1972	£60 000
1973	£60 000

This level is likely to continue in future years. The company has been advised by its agents that the likely return on investments of this nature is 10%.
6. The additional staff that would be required at head office to implement the plan, and the marketing effort that would be needed would cost in the region of £100 000 per annum.

After a lengthy discussion, the board accepted these proposals as the basis for developing the company. To finance the expenditure that it would entail the chairman proposed that the company should make a rights issue to raise £500 000 by an issue at 40s per share.

The financial director commented that he felt that the level of new funds envisaged (i.e., £500 000) would not be adequate for the purpose in view of the considerably higher level of sales that was being forecast and the continuing lock-up of funds in properties. He thought that the figure required would be in the region of £900 000 to £1 million. He also pointed out that since the 1965 Finance Act it would be cheaper to borrow the money rather than to raise it from shareholders.

Mr Carless objected to this proposal. He argued that it would add considerably to the risks of the business, and said, 'I like to sleep at nights and not worry where the next £1000 is coming from!'

After considerable argument, the financial director was requested to explore the possibility of borrowing £1 million and to set out the effect that the alternative financing proposals would have on the company and its shareholders.

The financial director's report which he presented to the board on the 4 September 1968 outlined the following three proposals:

1. To borrow an additional £1 million in the form of a 20 year debenture carrying an interest rate of 8%. This would be secured on the assets of the business except that it would rank after the existing mortgage in respect of freehold land and buildings.
2. To issue a debenture of £1·4 million at an interest rate of $7\frac{1}{2}\%$, using a part of the proceeds to repay the existing mortgage. Over the life of the debentures, the amount outstanding would be reduced by £50 000 per year by annual drawings commencing in the year 1974 and through to the year of repayment of the remaining balance outstanding, 1988.

(Under both 1 and 2 above the interest would be payable in semi-annual instalments on 1 July and 1 January.)

3. To make a right issue of 500 000 new ordinary shares at a subscription price of 40s per share.

The financial director assessed the capital requirements of the company over the period as follows:

1. Initial design and marketing, £200 000	
Less tax relief, i.e.	£120 000
2. Premises and Plant	250 000
3. Investment in Properties over 5 years	280 000
4. Estimated increase in:	
Work in progress	200 000
Debtors	100 000
	950 000
5. Contingencies and costs of issue	50 000
	£1 000 000

Questions
1. How would you supplement the financial director's report with the appropriate analysis of the effect of each of the financing alternatives on the return on equity?
2. How would you assess the risks involved?
3. Comment on any other aspects of the problem which you think are relevant.

Exhibit 20.1 Thompsons (Contractors) Limited
Balance Sheet as at 31 December 1967

	£ 000s	£ 000s
Fixed Assets		
Freehold Land and Buildings		645
Plant and Machinery at Cost	2837	
(Depreciation Rate 15% of Reducing Balance)		
Less Depreciation	1473	
		1364
Vehicles at Cost	730	
(Depreciation Rate 20 % of Reducing Balance)		
Less Depreciation	383	
		347
		2356
Current Assets		
Stocks on hand and Work in progress for Clients,		
Less Progress Payments Claimed	1026	
Debtors	898	
Cash	112	
		2036
		4392
Less *Current Liabilities*		
Creditors and Subcontractors	1573	
Taxation due 1.1.68	110	
Dividend Payable	137	
		1820
Funds Employed		£2572
Share Capital: Authorized and Issued 1 100 000		
£1 Ordinary Shares		1100
Capital Reserves		547
Revenue Reserves		397
		2044
Future Tax		128
5% Mortgage Secured on Freehold Properties Repayable 1971		400
		£2572

Exhibit 20.2 Thompsons (Contractors) Limited
Profit and Loss Account for Year to 31 December 1967

	£ 000s
Sales	5516
Contract and Site Costs (Including Depreciation of Plant)	4695
Gross Profit on Contracts	821
Head Office Expenses (Including £25 000 Depreciation on Equipment Used at HO)	480
Net Operating Profit	341
Interest on Mortgage	20
Profit before tax	321
Corporation Tax	128
	193
Dividend 12½%	137
Profit retained	56
Retained Profit from Previous Years	341
Retained Profit Carried Forward	£397

21

The De La Rue Company Limited (A)*

Charles Manning, a financial analyst with a well-known firm of stockbrokers, was about to make an assessment of the De La Rue Company based on their most recently published accounts. His assessment was to be used as a basis on which advice would be given to clients. One of the principal questions that he would need to decide would be whether the company should be recommended as an investment for income or for capital appreciation. He decided to start by computing various ratios and comparing them with those that he had computed from the various years' accounts.

Questions
1. Compute the financial ratios and percentages for 1963 to 1964 from the information given in the consolidated financial statements. Use the blank spaces provided in Exhibit 21.4.
2. Evaluate your results for 1963 to 1964 in comparison with the ratios calculated by Charles Manning for 1962 to 1963. What do you consider the significant ratios in each group?
3. Consider what additional information Charles Manning might need to evaluate the financial position of the company.
4. How do you appraise the opportunity of investment in the company as an ordinary or preference shareholder? For regular income? For long-term capital growth?

*Case material of the Management Case Research Programme, Cranfield, Bedford, England, and prepared as a basis for class discussion. This case was made possible through the cooperation of The De La Rue Company Limited. Reproduced by kind permission of the Cranfield School of Management.

111

Exhibit 21.1 The De La Rue Company Limited (A)*

DE LA RUE
'Steady Confidence in a Future Full of Challenge . . .'

Profits

The net profit attributable to De La Rue shareholders after taxes and outside shareholders' interests has increased from £933 189 to £1 048 612. The profits before tax of the four operating subsidiary groups are as follows: Formica International Limited £1 847 409 against £1 665 645; Thomas De La Rue International Limited £643 518 against £845 030; Thomas Potterton Limited £635 584 against £576 852 and Frigistor Group (European Interests) £31 615 (loss) as against £13 394 (loss).

The Directors recommend an increase in the Authorized Capital from £6 500 000 to £7 500 000 by the creation of a further 2 000 000 Ordinary shares of 10s 0d each to provide for the use of the technique of share exchange in appropriate cases of acquisition. No such acquisition involving an exchange of shares is at present under consideration.

Formica Group. The Formica Group of companies has had an excellent year and earnings before taxation have passed the figure achieved in the record year 1959/60.

Thomas De La Rue Group. This group of companies, operating in the specialized fields of security printing and physical security has had a disappointing year, but the old established, highly progressive banknote business had an excellent year's trading.

Thomas Potterton Limited. In spite of some further losses in Australia, this has been another highly successful year for Pottertons.

Frigistor Group. The Board feel that the risks involved in this new business are justifiable and I hardly need to assure shareholders that regular progress reports will be made on the status of this investment.

De La Rue Bull Machines Limited. Last year was the best since the company's formation in June 1959.

The Future

By recommending an increased dividend (1s 6d against 1s 4½d), after a year in which profits before taxation have remained under pressure, the Board has demonstrated its confidence in the immediate future. A recovery in overall profit margins is on the way and will, I hope, be maintained by the elimination of losses in some of our newer ventures. Some of this improvement is expected to occur this year and with continued progress by our established profit-earners there is every reason to look for improved results by the Group as a whole at the end of the year.

As to the more distant future, I can only reaffirm the steady confidence we have always held and demonstrated by our willingness to go ahead with risk-taking projects when ever and where ever we have judged those risks to be acceptable and the possible rewards good enough.

*This Exhibit is an extract from a review by A. G. Norman which appeared in *The Times* of 30 July 1964.

Salient Features for the Year Ended 28 March 1964

	1964 £	1963 £
Group Turnover:		
Home Sales	13 050 000	9 861 000
Export Sales from the UK	7 331 000	6 895 000
Sales by Overseas Companies	10 074 000	7 991 000
	30 455 000	24 747 000
Group Profit before Tax	2 598 000	2 755 000
Profit before Tax as a Percentage of Turnover	8·5%	11·1%
Group Capital Employed	20 863 000	15 659 000
Profit before Tax as a Percentage of Capital Employed	13·8%	19·5%
Profit after Tax Attributable to the Ordinary Shareholders	1 038 000	922 000
Ordinary Dividends (less Income Tax)		
Interim paid—6d per Share (1963 6d per Share)	170 000	170 000
Final proposed—1s per Share (1963 10½d per Share)	340 000	298 000
Total Dividend	£510 000	£468 000
Cover for Dividend on Ordinary Shares	2·0	2·0

Exhibit 21.2 The De La Rue Company Limited (A)
The De La Rue Company Limited and Subsidiary Companies
Consolidated Balance Sheet as at 28 March 1964 (£ 000s)

	1964		1963	
	£	£	£	£
CAPITAL EMPLOYED				
Preference Capital				
3½% Cumulative Preference Stock		500		500
Ordinary Shareholders' Interests				
Ordinary Shares of 10s each	5556		5556	
Share Premium Account	—		67	
Capital Reserves	1186		808	
Undistributed Profits	4396		4117	
		11 138		10 548
Outside Shareholder's Interests		4943		3862
Future Taxation		588		725
Long-Term Liabilities		3694		25
		£20 863		£15 660
EMPLOYMENT OF CAPITAL				
Fixed Assets				
Land, Buildings, and Plant	11 701		8086	
Licences, Goodwill, etc.	2428		1665	
Subsidiary Companies not Consolidated	410		95	
Trade Investments	1260		974	
		15 799		10 820
Current Assets				
Stocks	5600		4946	
Debtors and Bills	7186		6318	
Cash and Deposits	1973		1860	
	14 759		13 124	
Current Liabilities				
Creditors and Bills	5605		4472	
Current Tax	554		631	
Overdraft and S/T Loans	3196		2883	
Dividends Unpaid	340		298	
	9695		8284	
Net Current Assets		5064		4840
		£20 863		£15 660

Exhibit 21.3 The De La Rue Company Limited (A)
The De La Rue Company Limited and Subsidiary Companies

Consolidated Profit and Loss Account for the 52 weeks ending 28 March 1964
(£000s)

	1964		1963	
	£	£	£	£
Net Sales		30 455		24 747
Less Cost of Sales		27 659*		21 972*
Trading Profit		2795		2775
Long-Term Interest Paid	129		2	
Short-Term Interest Paid Less Dividends Received	68	197	18	20
Group Profit Before Tax		2598		2755
Taxation		1026		1421
Group Profit After Tax		1572		1334
Profit Attributable to Outside Shareholders		523		401
Profit Attributable to the De La Rue Company Limited		1049		933
Preference Dividends (net)		11		11
Profit Attributable to Ordinary Shareholders		1038		922
Ordinary Dividends (net) 1s 6d per Share (1963 1s 4½d per Share)		510		468
Profit Retained in the Group		528		454
Balance of Undistributed Profit		3868		3663
Total Undistributed Profit		£4396		£4117

*Including operating expenses.

Exhibit 21.4

The De La Rue Company Limited (A)

			1962/63 £ 000s		1963/64 £ 000s
A.	*Ratios Appraising Liquidity*				
A1	Current ratio	Current assets : current liabilities	13 124 : 8284	= 1·6 : 1	
A2	Acid test	Quick assets : current liabilities	8178 : 8284	= 0·99 : 1	
A3	Debt ratio	Total debt : total assets	8309 : 23 944	= 1 : 2·9	
A4	Owners equity/total debt	Owners equity : total debt	11 048 : 8309	= 1·3 : 1	
B.	*Ratios Appraising Funds Management (Turnover Relationships)*				
B1	Collection period	$\dfrac{\text{Debtors}}{\text{Net sales}} \times 365$ days = collection period	$\dfrac{6318}{24\,747} \times 365$ days	= 93 days	
B2	Debtors/sales (percentage)	$\dfrac{\text{Debtors}}{\text{Net sales}} \times 100\%$	$\dfrac{6318}{24\,747} \times 100\%$	= 25·57	
B3	Stock (inventory) turnover	$\dfrac{\text{Cost of sales}}{\text{Ending inventory}} =$ Stock turnover	$\dfrac{21\,972}{4946}$	= 4·4 times	
B4	Inventory/sales (percentage)	$\dfrac{\text{Ending inventory}}{\text{Net sales}} \times 100\%$	$\dfrac{4946}{24\,747} \times 100\%$	= 20%	
B5	Number of days sales in the inventory	$\dfrac{\text{Inventory}}{\text{Sales}} \times 36$ days = Number of days of sales held in inventory	$\dfrac{4946}{24\,747} \times 365$	= 73 days	
B6	Creditors payment period	$\dfrac{\text{Creditors}}{\text{Cost of sales}^{1}} \times 365$ days = Number of days of credit received from suppliers	$\dfrac{4472}{21\,972} \times 365$	= 73 days	
B7	Sales/assets (measure of activity)	$\dfrac{\text{Sales}}{\text{Assets}} =$ Number of times assets are turned over	$\dfrac{24\,747}{23\,944}$	= 1·1 times	
B8	Sales/fixed assets	$\dfrac{\text{Net sales}}{\text{Fixed assets}} =$ Number of times fixed assets are turned over	$\dfrac{24\,747}{10\,820}$	= 2·3 times	
C.	*Ratio Appraising Profitability Related to Assets*				
C1	Return on profits—net profit	$\dfrac{\text{Net profit + interest on long term debt}}{\text{Total assets}} \times 100\%$ = rate of profitability of the assets	$\dfrac{1334 + 2}{23\,994} \times 100\%$	= 5·6%	
C2	Return on total owners equity (net worth)	$\dfrac{\text{Net profit}}{\text{Total owners equity}} \times 100\% = \dfrac{\text{rate of profitability of owners investment}}{\text{in the business}}$	$\dfrac{1334}{11\,048} \times 100\%$	= 12·1%	
C3	Return on ordinary shareholders investment	$\dfrac{\text{Net profit—outside shareholders profits—preference share dividend}}{\text{Owners equity or ordinary shareholders}} \times 100\%$ = rate of profitability of ordinary shareholders investment	$\dfrac{1334 - 401 - 11}{10\,548} \times 100\%$	= 8·7%	

Exhibit 21.4 (continued)

D. Ratios Appraising Profitability Related to Sales (Profit Margins)

D1 Gross profit return on sales — $\dfrac{\text{Gross profit}^2}{\text{Net sales}} \times 100\%$ = Gross profit on sales = $\dfrac{2775}{24\,747} \times 100\%$ = 11·2%

D2 Net profit³ related to sales — $\dfrac{\text{Net profit}}{\text{Net sales}} \times 100\%$ = Net profit on sales = $\dfrac{922}{24\,747} \times 100\%$ = 3·7%

D3 Operating expenses related to sales — $\dfrac{\text{Operating expenses}}{\text{Net sales}} \times 100\%$ = Operating expenses on sales = $\dfrac{\text{Not known}}{24\,747} \times 100\%$ =

D4 Cost of sales related to sales — $\dfrac{\text{Cost of sales}^1}{\text{Net sales}} \times 100\%$ = Cost of goods sold on sales = $\dfrac{21\,972}{24\,747} \times 100\%$ = 88·8%

E. Ratios Appraising Investments

E1 Earnings per ordinary share — $\dfrac{\text{Net profit—outside shareholders profit—preference dividend}}{\text{Ordinary shares outstanding (number)}}$ = earnings per ordinary share = $\dfrac{1334 - 401 - 11}{11\,112}$ = 1s 8d per ord. share after tax⁴ (before tax 2s 9d)

E2 Earnings yield on ordinary share — $\dfrac{\text{Earnings per ordinary share (after tax)}}{\text{Market price per ordinary share}^5} \times 100\%$ = yield on ordinary share = $\dfrac{\text{1s 8d}}{\text{41s 0d}} \times 100\%$ = 4·1%

E3 Dividend yield per ordinary share — $\dfrac{\text{Dividend per ordinary share (net)}}{\text{Market price per ordinary share}^5} \times 100\%$ = yield on market price = $\dfrac{\text{1s 4½d}}{\text{41s 0d}} \times 100\%$ = 3·4%

E4 Number of times dividend covered — $\dfrac{\text{Earnings per ordinary share}}{\text{Dividend per ordinary share}}$ = number of times covered = $\dfrac{\text{2s 9d}}{\text{1s 4½d}}$ = 2 times = 2 times

E5 Nominal value per ordinary share — Nominal value per ordinary share given in the balance sheet = 10s 0d

E6 Book value per ordinary share — $\dfrac{\text{Owners equity less nominal value of preference shares}}{\text{Number of ordinary shares}}$ = Book value per ordinary share = $\dfrac{11\,048 - 500}{11\,112}$ = 19s per share

Notes:
¹Includes operating expenses.
²As gross profit is not shown in these accounts, trading profit is used (this includes expenses).
³Profit attributable to ordinary shareholders used in place of net profit.
⁴To convert after tax figure to before tax figure we must adjust for deduction of 7s 9d in £1. We therefore multiply $\dfrac{£1}{£1 - 7s\ 9d}$
⁵Assume price for 1963/64 is 38s 0d.

22

The De La Rue Company Limited (B)*

After Charles Manning had finished computing the financial ratios for the De La Rue Company (see De La Rue Company (A)), he looked at the notes to the accounts (given as Exhibits 22.1 and 22.2) and computed his own funds flow and projected balance sheet for the following year, using the ratios he had just worked out.

Questions
1. How does the additional data provided in this case affect your appraisal of the De La Rue Company Limited as an investment opportunity?
2. Prepare a funds flow statement, and compare your figures with those given in Exhibit 22.3. How do you account for any differences?
3. What significant transactions are revealed by your funds flow statement for 1963 to 1964?
4. Can you use financial ratios and percentages to forecast the balance sheet of the company for 1964 to 1965 and 1965 to 1966, based upon an increase in sales estimate of 20%?

*Case Material of the Management Case Research Programme, Cranfield, Bedford, England, and prepared as a basis for class discussion. This case was made possible through the cooperation of The De La Rue Company Limited. Reproduced by kind permission of the Cranfield School of Management.

Exhibit 22.1 The De La Rue Company Limited (B)

Notes on Balance Sheet as at 28 March 1964 (£ 000s)

These notes are part of the accounts, and are given to conform with the requirements of the Companies Act, 1948.

	1964 £	1963 £
1. *SHARE CAPITAL* At 28 March 1964, the Authorized Capital of the Company was:		
Preference Stock	500	500
12 000 000 Ordinary Shares of 10s each	6000	6000
	6500	6500

	£
2. *SHARE PREMIUM ACCOUNT* At 30 March 1963	66
Less Discount and Part of Expenses of Debenture Issue	66
	—

	Group £	The De La Rue Co Ltd £
3. *CAPITAL RESERVES*		
At 30 March 1963	808	1545
Add		
Surplus Arising on Revaluation of Certain Freehold Properties in the UK	318	—
Transfer from Undistributed Profits (See Note 4 to Consolidated Profit and Loss Account)	235	—
	1361	1545
Deduct		
Net Deficit on Capital Transactions and Balance of Debenture Issue Costs	36	2
Amount Written Off Investments in a Subsidiary Company and Two Trade Investments	139	115
	175	117
	1186	1427

119

4. LICENCES, GOODWILL, ETC. (At Cost
   Less Amounts Written Off)

	1964 £	1963 £
Licences, Patents, and Trademarks	250	246
Goodwill and Premium Paid on Acquisition	1991	1354
Preliminary and Preproduction Expenses	187	65
	2428	1665

5. SUBSIDIARY COMPANIES

(a) The directors consider it necessary that the accounts of overseas subsidiaries are prepared to 31 December, so that group accounts can be prepared without delay.

(b) Foreign currencies have been converted into sterling as follows:
Fixed Assets at the exchange rates ruling at the date of acquisition.
Current Assets and Liabilities at exchange rates ruling on 31 December 1963.

In the case of Brazil, current assets, current liabilities and additions to fixed assets have been converted at the average of the relevant fixed and market rates during the year.

(c) *Subsidiary Companies not Consolidated*

	1964 £	1963 £
Shares at Cost Less Amounts (Written Off)	338	67
Amounts Owing	72	28
	410	95

(d) Nine subsidiary companies have not been consolidated because, in the opinion of the directors, consolidation would be of no real value to the members of the company owing to the insignificant amount involved. Five subsidiary companies have not traded since control was obtained. Four subsidiary companies have traded for only part of the year, resulting in net aggregate losses, so far as concerns the members of the De La Rue Company Limited, of £3190.

6. TRADE INVESTMENTS

Trade investments in the group are stated at cost, less amounts written off, and include loans amounting to £258 688 (parent company £188 993).

7. STOCK

A concise statement of the basis used for the valuation of stock is not practicable due to the diversity of the activities of the group, but the amount shown has been determined for the whole of the stock at the balance sheet date on bases which are considered appropriate in the circumstances, and which have been consistently applied.

8. *BANK OVERDRAFT AND SHORT-TERM LOANS*
Bank and other loans to two overseas subsidiary companies amounting to
£64 328 (1963 £59 224) are secured against those companies' land, buildings, and machinery.

9. *CAPITAL COMMITMENTS*
Capital commitments at the balance sheet dates amount to £1 240 953
(1963 £1 736 175), of which £853 (1963 £356) was attributable to the
parent company.

10. *CONTINGENT LIABILITIES*
There were contingent liabilities at 28 March 1964, or at the dates of the
subsidiary companies' balance sheets, as follows:
(a) Guarantees to banks and others of £1 332 660 (1963 £944 530) of
which £1 190 118 (1963 £750 000) was guaranteed by the parent
company.
(b) Bills of Exchange discounted by overseas subsidiary companies
£1 181 730 (1963 £1 050 201).
(c) A liability in respect of part paid shares in subsidiary companies
amounting to £311 040 (1963 £641 000).
(d) Forward contracts for raw materials entered into by a subsidiary
company amounted to £554 376 (1963 nil).

11. *LAND, BUILDINGS, AND PLANT*

	1964		
	Cost or as revalued	Deprecia-tion	Balance
GROUP	£	£	£
Land and Buildings	5229	753	4476
Plant and Equipment	12 479	5254	7225
	17 708	6007	11 701
THE DE LA RUE COMPANY LIMITED			
Land and Buildings	227	52	175
Plant and Equipment	122	83	39
	349	135	214
	1963		
GROUP	£	£	£
Land and Buildings	3606	655	2951
Plant and Equipment	9430	4295	5135
	13 036	4950	8086

THE DE LA RUE COMPANY LIMITED

Land and Buildings	198	44	154
Plant and Equipment	122	82	40
	320	126	194

The fixed assets are included at original cost to the company or its subsidiaries, with the exception of certain freehold properties of two subsidiaries which have been professionally valued. The amount set aside for depreciation consequently include amounts provided before formation of subsidiaries and by subsidiaries before their acquisition by the company. No provision has been made in the accounts of certain subsidiary companies for depreciation on freehold land and buildings, because, in the opinion of the directors, no such provision is necessary.

Exhibit 22.2 The De La Rue Company Limited (B)
Notes on the Consolidated Profit and Loss Account (£ 000s)

These notes are part of the Accounts and are given to conform with the requirements of the Companies Act, 1948.

	1964		1963	
	£	£	£	£
1. THE TRADING PROFIT OF THE GROUP is arrived at after deducting:				
(a) Depreciation		1051		848
(b) Remuneration of the Directors of the De La Rue Company Limited:				
Fees as Directors of Parent Company	11		10	
Remuneration for Management	99		87	
Pensions	8		7	
		118		104
(c) Auditor's Remuneration (UK Companies)		11		9
and after adding:				
Royalties received in respect of previous years		—		150

	1964	1963
	£	£
2. INTEREST AND DIVIDENDS		
Debenture Interest	123	—
Other Long-Term Interest	6	2
	129	2
Short-Term Interest and Charges (Net)	138	72
Less Dividend and Interests from Trade Investments	70	54
	68	18

3. *TAXATION*
   (a) No provision is made for UK taxation which might be payable in the event of distribution of profits retained in the overseas subsidiaries.
   (b) The charge for taxation consists of the following:

	1964 £	1963 £
UK Taxation		
Income Tax	332	577
Profits Tax	160	258
	492	835
Overseas Taxation	534	586
	1026	1421

   (c) The UK Taxation charge has been reduced by £287 000 (1963 £146 000) as a result of taxation relief from investment allowances.

   In addition, taxation relief to an amount of £80 000 has arisen from the additional annual allowances on capital expenditure in development areas in the UK which are in excess of the normal allowances granted in other areas. This amount has not been deducted from the current taxation charge, but has been carried forward and has been included in 'Future Taxation' on the balance sheet, by way of an equalization reserve.

4. *UNDISTRIBUTED PROFITS OF SUBSIDIARY COMPANIES*

	£	£	Amounts transferred to Capital Reserve £
At 30 March 1963		1961	
Less Capitalization by Subsidiary, Transfer to Capital Reserve	199		199
Overseas Taxes on Capitalization	13		
		212	
		1749	
Profits Retained in Current Year		520	
		2269	
Less Other Transfers to Capital Reserve		35	35
		2234	234

Exhibit 22.3 The De La Rue Company Limited (B)

Source and Use of Total Funds 1960–1964 (£ 000s)

	Five Year Summary	1964	1963	1962	1961	1960
Cash and Short-Term Deposits at Beginning of Year	801	1860	178	496	1727	801
Add						
Total Profits Retained and Reinvested	3561	788	688	614	721	750
Depreciation Charged Against Profits	3707	1051	848	688	596	524
Additional Funds:						
De La Rue Shareholders	3797	—	2778	—	—	1019
Outside Shareholders	1691	806	190	—	309	386
Debenture and Long-Term Liabilities	3694	3669	25	—	—	—
Increase in Loans and Bank Overdrafts	3196	313	875	1550	458	—
	20 447	8487	5582	3348	3811	3480
Deduct						
Capital and Investment Expenditure	14 241	5956	2417	1978	2460	1430
Increase in Net Current Assets and Liabilities (Other than Cash and Loans)	4233	558	1305	1192	855	323
	18 474	6514	3722	3170	3315	1753
Cash and Short-Term Deposits at End of Year	1973	1973	1860	178	496	1727

Exhibit 22.4 The De La Rue Company Limited (B)
Subsidiary and Associated Companies

SUBSIDIARY COMPANIES

Thomas De La Rue International Limited
Thomas De La Rue and Company Limited
Thomas De La Rue S.A. Industrias Graficas
Security Express Limited
Thomas De La Rue de Columbia SA
Thomas De La Rue Incorporated
Compania Mexicana Impresora de Valores SA
De La Rue Mexicana, SA
Thomas De La Rue Engineering Limited
De La Rue Instruments Limited
Thomas De La Rue AG
Independent Security Consultants Limited
Staderini Carte-Calori SpA
Impresora Internacional de Valores SA (Industrial y Commercial)
De La Rue Transportadora De Valores SA
Société Nouvelle d'Imprimerie Bernard Frères SA

Formica International Limited
Formica Limited
Société Anonyme Formica
Formica (NZ) Limited
Formica Plastics Pty Limited
Formica GmbH
Formica Belgium SA
Formica Espanola SA
Formica Nederland NV
J. & H. Rosenberg Limited
Tyne Board Company Limited
Tyne Timber and Veneers Limited

Thomas Potterton Limited
Potterton Industries Pty Limited
Inferation Limited
Abair SA

Frigistor Holdings Limited
De La Rue Frigistor Limited
De La Rue Frigistor SA
Frigistor Laboratories Limited

ASSOCIATED COMPANIES
De La Rue Bull Machines Limited
Formica India Limited
Pakistan Security Printing Corporation Limited
International Card Company Limited
Nigeria Security Printing and Minting Company Limited
Securitas Express AG

125

Exhibit 22.5   The De La Rue Company Limited (B)

General Information

	The World	UK and W Europe	Asia and Far East	Australasia	The Americas	Africa	Middle East, USSR, and E Europe
Number of employees 1964	10 930	8395	1314	338	883	—	—
Number of shares held 1964	11 112 000	11 055 535	25 138	3992	16 441	10 749	145
Total sales by area £ 000s:							
1964	30 455	21 554	3713	1765	2650	480	293
1963	24 747	16 942	3507	1557	1970	546	225
1962	21 909	14 340	4229	1226	1041	640	433
1961	18 542	12 882	2326	1215	1582	349	188
1960	17 056	12 788	2182	817	538	415	316
Total capital employed in the group by areas:							
1964	20 863	17 672	491	981	1559	160	—
1963	15 659	13 727	200	915	817	—	—
1962	12 089	10 246	200	874	769	—	—
1961	11 311	9563	200	786	762	—	—
1960	10 140	8724	199	762	455	—	—

23

The De La Rue Company Limited (C1)*

After preparing a funds flow statement, Manning returned to notes to the accounts and the chairman's statement (Exhibit 23.1) and examined them to see what significant transactions they revealed. He also compared the De La Rue share index performance with other companies (Exhibit 23.3) and that of the Economist Extel Indicator (Exhibit 23.4).

Questions
1. What transactions do the notes to the accounts reveal?
2. How do these transactions affect your assessment of the company?
3. Would you invest in the company and with what object? How has your judgement changed during this series of cases?
4. What is the significance of the various components of a set of published accounts?

Exhibit 23.1 The De La Rue Company Limited (C1)

Extracts from the Review by the Chairman
The Year 1963/64. The final results for the past year are very much in line with the indications given in the quarterly statements issued by the board during the course of the year. Group sales have increased by 23% and, although the trading profits of the main subsidiaries have not increased commensurately, they have not fallen in amount. Group profit before taxation has fallen somewhat below the record figure achieved in 1962/63. The net profit attributable to De La Rue shareholders after the deduction of taxes and outside shareholders' interests has increased from £933 189 to £1 048 612.

*Case material of the Management Case Research Programme, Cranfield, Bedford, England, and prepared as a basis for class discussion. This case was made possible through the cooperation of The De La Rue Company Limited. Reproduced by kind permission of the Cranfield School of Management.

The turnover and profits before tax of the four operating subsidiary groups, with comparable figures for 1962/63, are as follows:

| | 1963/64 | | 1962/63 | |
	Turnover £	Profits before tax £	Turnover £	Profits before tax £
Formica International Limited	15 432 944	1 847 409	12 644 000	1 665 645
Thomas De La Rue International Limited	9 057 022	643 518	7 429 176	845 030
Thomas Potterton Limited	5 935 201	635 584	4 667 613	576 852
Frigistor Group (European Interests)	29 610	(31 615)	6022	(13 394)
	30 454 777	3 094 896	24 746 811	3 074 133
From which *Deduct the De La Rue Company Limited*				
Management Expenses		389 401		344 834
Debenture Interest (gross)		122 849		—
Interest Received		15 573		25 820
		496 677		319 014
Profits Before Tax		2 598 219		2 755 119

This year, in setting out for the first time the turnover and profits of each of the main operating subsidiary companies, the aim has been to let shareholders know what contribution to profits comes from each part of the business. Sales and profits or losses of associated companies in which the De La Rue Company or its subsidiaries hold 50% or less of the issued shares are not included in the above figures. Where any dividends have been received from such companies, these have been included. Where appropriate in this review, I shall make special reference to the status of any large investment in associated companies such as De La Rue Bull Machines Limited and the Frigistor group.

It will be noticed that the expenses of managing the group have been shown separately this year and that debenture interest is a new charge which, in a full year will amount to £172 500. Management expenses for the year under review show an increase of some £44 000; this arises, almost entirely, from non-recurring expenses chargeable to the parent company for the 150th anniversary advertising and publicity activities which have been well received in all countries in which De La Rue companies are operating.

In making comparisons with the results of 1962/63, shareholders will remember that last year the trading profit of the group was increased by the inclusion of £150 000 of deferred royalties from an overseas licensee. But even after making allowances for this, the overall profit margin dropped back from 11·9% in 1961/62 to 10·5% last year and to 8·5% in the year under review. Reference has been made to this circumstance in every quarterly statement during the past twelve months and the figures in the above table show clearly that, while the Formica International and Thomas Potterton figures are highly satisfactory, Thomas De La Rue International, our security printing subsidiary, has experienced a substantial drop in profits; this arises mainly from the recent expansion and extension of that company's investment and trading activities in overseas markets, particularly in the United States of America, which cannot be expected to yield profits in the early period of their existence. Moreover, the prices of many of our products have been reduced, particularly in the Potterton and Formica companies, not only to meet competitive situations, but also to attract the greater volume of orders which our modernized plants demand. There is also the effect of the payment of interest on the £3-million Debenture Stock issued last August. The proceeds of this issue have been put to work mainly in new ventures in Thomas De La Rue & Company Limited and in J. & H. Rosenberg Limited, which was purchased by Formica International Limited on 1 August last.

I shall refer in greater detail to the situation of each operating group at a later stage in this review. At this point I wish to draw attention to the figure of £1 048 612 net profit attributable to De La Rue shareholders compared with £933 189 for 1962/63. The increase is largely due to the incidence of taxation allowances arising from our heavy capital expenditure in the United Kingdom, which amounted to some £2·6 million against £1·4 million in the previous year. A large part of this expenditure was made in what are popularly known as 'free depreciation areas' and, therefore, attracted allowances in excess of normal levels. However, in computing the amount to be charged for tax in any financial year, the board thinks it prudent to carry forward against the taxation charge in future years any benefit that may accrue from 'free depreciation area' allowances in excess of the recognized annual allowances; this has been done with respect to the tax charge in the year under review.

Dividend Policy

The board of directors has weighed carefully all the factors which influence a sound dividend policy and, although the increased profits available for distribution this year are mainly due to higher tax allowances, the outlook for the group as a whole is sufficiently promising to warrant the board recommending a modest increase in dividend to a total of 1s 6d per share as against 1s 4½d per share last year. If this is approved by shareholders at the annual general meeting on 29 July, the dividend will be covered more than twice, and the profits ploughed back into the business will amount to £527 436 as against £454 551 in 1962/63.

Balance Sheet

The balance sheet which accompanies this review, differs in some quite substantial respects from the balance sheet for the previous year.

The total capital employed in the group has increased since March 1963 from just over £15½ million to just under £21 million; of this increase some

129

£5 million is attributable to fixed assets and £200 000 to net current assets. Under the heading fixed assets, £3·6 million of the total increase has been employed in Land, Buildings, Plant, and Equipment, mainly connected with the new banknote factory at Gateshead, further expansion by Potterton at Warwick, the new Research Centre at Maidenhead, the Formica expansion that has taken place in the United Kingdom, France, and Australia, and through Formica International's recent acquisition of J. & H. Rosenburg. The expansion by Thomas De La Rue International in the United States is also reflected under this heading.

The increase under Licences, Goodwill, etc., arises mainly from premiums paid as a result of acquisitions made by Formica Limited and Thomas De La Rue International during the year in the United Kingdom, in Europe, and in the United States.

A net increase of some £300 000 in trade investments results from a further investment by the group in De La Rue Bull Machines Limited, and from the investments by Thomas De La Rue International Limited in Nigeria, and in the playing card interests of the business in Europe.

The increase in net current assets are largely the result of greater stocks and an increase in debtors, offset by an increase in creditors and the small overall increase in bank overdrafts and short-term loans; these variations are the result of the increase in the turnover of the group as a whole.

This substantial increase in the employment of capital throughout the group has been balanced by the debenture stock of £3 000 000 issued last August and by the contribution from outside shareholders during the course of the year under review, of the amount of £1 million. In addition, there has been the continuing policy of ploughing back profits, and the use of the amount provided for depreciation which this year reached a figure of over £1 million. During the course of the year, there were some transactions affecting both the capital reserves and the undistributed profits. The cost of the debenture stock issue, which amounted to £68 548, has been charged against the share premium account and capital reserves. The share premium account now disappears.

Certain freehold properties were revalued during the year and the resulting surplus of just over £300 000 was used to write off a net loss on the sale of some fixed assets and to write down some trade investments. The total result of these transactions has been an increase of capital reserves by some £145 000. Finally, one of our overseas subsidiary companies increased its capital by capitalizing undistributed profits, and this has resulted in just under £200 000 being transferred from the group's undistributed profits to capital reserves.

Finance Company

As has already been reported, The De La Rue Finance Company Limited was formed during the course of the year to assist the marketing activities of companies within the group. It is too early to report on the operations of this small unit, but it has now begun to provide financial assistance on a modest scale to Thomas De La Rue Engineering Limited. In the future, it is expected that De La Rue Bull Machines Limited will be able to use the facilities provided by this company.

Finance

The programme of capital expenditure in the year ahead, while not matching that carried out in the year under review, is expected to top the £3 million mark. The greater part of this expenditure will be overseas.

The directors are of the opinion that the cash flow being generated within the group and the facilities already available from bankers throughout the world will be sufficient to meet our financial requirements during the current year. Projects and acquisitions may arise in the future which could require cash or shares, and the Directors think it advisable to recommend to shareholders an increase in the authorized capital from the present figure of £6 500 000 to £7 500 000 by the creation of a further 2 000 000 Ordinary shares of 10s each to provide for the use of the technique of share exchange in appropriate cases of acquisition. Although no such acquisition involving an exchange of shares is at present under consideration, shareholders will be asked to approve the necessary special resolution at the annual general meeting.

Formica International Limited

The Formica group of companies has had an excellent year and earnings before taxation have passed the figure achieved in the record year 1959/60. Profit on sales has remained constant at about 12% and earnings as a percentage of capital employed have risen from 16% to 17%.

The background to this good performance is one of strong international competition and falling prices; the remedies applied have been expansion of sales and marketing efforts, modernization of equipment, the withdrawal of unprofitable products, and continuous emphasis on measures to raise productivity and to cut costs. Much better results from our German company under its new management team have made the greatest single contribution to this overall improvement on last year's results, and there is now a fair expectation that during the current year the German company will show a trading profit for the first time. In the home and export markets, Formica Limited has increased the range of its products by introducing many variants, both in specification and design, in the range of decorative laminates. There have also been increases in the sales of all products, including industrial laminates which are sold to electrical, radio, television, and electronic users in the United Kingdom and overseas. The acquisition of J. & H. Rosenberg, which made a modest contribution to profits this year, has opened up a new opportunity to supply the fast-expanding building and construction industries; the chipboard production capacity of this unit has been doubled in the last twelve months in expectation of an expanding, though highly competitive, market in the United Kingdom in both the furnishing and building industries.

In France, Australia, New Zealand, and Spain, capable and enthusiastic managements are contributing their share to the profits of Formica International. Formica India Limited will start production this year. Marketing companies in Holland and Belgium strengthened their position in their respective markets. In all these companies, and in the United Kingdom, there will be further increases in the product range during the current year and the outlook for Formica International Limited is full of promise.

131

The thermoplastic piping activity in Cricklewood has been closed down because it proved to be uneconomic for us to compete against raw material manufacturers possessing their own fabricating facilities. The thermoplastic container business has been transferred to the injection moulding and extruding factory at Glenrothes in Scotland, and this small but expanding unit is earning profits.

Thomas De La Rue International Limited

As I have already reported, this group of companies, operating in the specialized fields of security printing and physical security and investing in ten countries outside the United Kingdom has had a disappointing year in terms of profit, but the bald figures conceal the fact that the old established but highly progressive banknote business had an excellent year's trading. During the year the new Gateshead factory was being completed in readiness for the move from Leeds, and since the close of the financial year this major movement has been carried through efficiently and with human understanding, although, inevitably, it has involved a slowing up of production during the first quarter of the current year and this will be reflected in the figures which are issued at the time of the annual general meeting. However, by that time, the new factory will be working at almost full output and the results for the last threequarters of the year are expected to compensate largely for a low sales and profit figure in the first quarter.

The losses incurred in the United States, and to a lesser extent in Mexico and in the printing of documents other than banknotes in the United Kingdom, have been responsible for the overall drop in profits. Today, the United States interests of Thomas De La Rue International consist of a financial and security printing division in New York and Long Island, a similar enterprise in Houston, Texas, and a physical security company, Central Station Signals Inc., in New York. The acquisition of this last interest only took place after the close of the financial year. The amount at stake, including direct investment, local borrowings, and guarantees, is now just over £2 million. Of these three divisions, the two last named are already making profits but, for the time being, the printing division in New York, which is the largest unit at present, is responsible for an overall loss in our United States operations. The objective is to correct this situation in the next twelve months, but much will depend on the behaviour of the financial market in New York which, for the moment, is not being called upon to finance business expansion through new issues on the scale envisaged.

If a question mark has to remain over the New York printing company during 1964, it can be removed from Security Express Limited which, after four years of hard endeavour, is now a profitable and expanding concern. Indeed, we have now begun to look at the overseas market for a cash and bullion carrying service and a start has been made in Colombia, Switzerland, and Australia.

During the year, the Thomas De La Rue group started financial and security printing activities on a small scale in France, Italy, and Argentina and I shall report to shareholders on the progress of these new overseas ventures after they have had time to get into their stride.

As might be expected, there will now be a period of consolidation in this vigorous group—there may need to be some pruning, too, while present investments are brought into profitability, but this general policy will not be allowed to stifle constructive moves which can contribute to strength and profitability.

Thomas Potterton Limited

In spite of some further losses in Australia, this has been another highly successful year for Pottertons. Costs have risen slightly and prices have been reduced, but greater volume, new plant, improved methods, and higher productivity have combined to maintain returns on turnover and investment at an acceptable level.

The comforts of hot water and central heating supplied by fully automatic and thermostatically controlled appliances are being appreciated by rapidly increasing numbers of people in this country, and the Potterton company's response to this opportunity has been to plough back every year experience and profits into a wider range of reliable products. The year 1963/64 has seen introduction of a new range of large gas boilers for commercial and industrial premises together with a similar range of oil-fired boiler burner units and a new simplified and easily fixed gas boiler for heating combined with hot water for the home. Radiators, manufactured by Fisher & Ludlow Limited are now being sold through the same marketing outlets as the boilers.

All these products have found good acceptance in the United Kingdom market, and good progress is being made in a determined effort to get exports flowing. This is not as easy as it may seem, because specifications in some markets require redesign before marketing can begin. However, a start in penetrating the growing and highly competitive European market has been made by the acquisition of a marketing company developed by our successful agent in Belgium. A careful study has been made of other markets and shareholders will, I hope, hear of other Potterton export initiatives during the current year.

Potterton have embarked on an entirely new venture—Inferation Limited—which was acquired in July 1963, and which has been merged with the small Coolite refrigeration business to form a viable and largely autonomous Potterton subsidiary producing electrically operated appliances for the catering, brewing, and heating industries.

The Potterton group's management team has been strengthened to meet the challenge of a very promising future at home and overseas. Much of the strength of Potterton lies in the high technical content of its products and in a well-established programme of continuous development of new and better appliances and services to meet the growing needs of industrial and domestic consumers. With parallel development of modern marketing, selling, and servicing techniques, there is every reason to hope for continuity in the good performance of this group.

The Frigistor Group

During the year, we have undergone the nerve-testing experience which the Formica and Potterton businesses gave us nearly 20 years ago. A new product

133

searching for a new market must either be backed fully or dropped completely, and during this critical stage of development there are few guidelines for those who must take the decisions which can lead either to the promised land or to failure. Pioneers are, it is said, rarely as well rewarded as are those who follow when the ground is safe. We have considered all these things and have decided to feed the Frigistor business not only with more working capital but also with men, headed by a director of the De La Rue Company, Mr Roger Sawtell, who is now working in Montreal.

At present, we have a minority interest of just over 16% in the equity of the Canadian company and, in addition, have provided funds secured by a debenture amounting to $543 000 (Canadian). We have also undertaken to guarantee borrowings by the Canadian company up to a total of $550 000 (Canadian). The terms of the present debenture now provide us with the right to convert that debenture into shares of Frigistor Limited on the basis that, if the right is fully exercised, De La Rue's interest in the equity would be increased from some 16% to just over 90%. Moreover, when these financial arrangements were being negotiated, it was agreed that the control of the European interests of Frigistor Limited would be assumed by De La Rue.

We are writing off our interest in the development costs incurred in the early period of the company's existence.

In total, our interest in this business both in Canada and Europe, including the debenture and loans, now amounts to just over £400 000.

We can now begin to see some prospect of the rate of loss being reduced and eventually staunched completely, though, here again, a swing towards or away from the use of this new thermoelectric cooling device on the part of a few important customers in North America will eventually decide how long we must wait for volume sales and for the sight of the first profitable trading account. The board feels that the risks involved in this new business are justifiable, and I hardly need to assure shareholders that regular progress reports will be made on the status of this investment.

De La Rue Bull Machines Limited

The De La Rue stake in this associate company at the end of the financial year amounted to £1 375 000 in the form of subscribed capital and loans guaranteed by the De La Rue Company. Last year was the best since the company's formation in June 1959; growing sales have justified the establishment of sales offices in Glasgow, Manchester, and Birmingham, as well as London, and, after taking into account the availability of new additions to the Bull range of equipment in the very near future, it is possible to see the break-even point being reached some time in the year 1965/66. The outlook could be radically altered by the outcome of present negotiations which our partners in France, Compagnie des Machines Bull (CMB), are conducting with other French companies, the French Government and the General Electric Company of the United States. What is becoming increasingly clear is the likely emergence in the foreseeable future of less than half a dozen very large and powerful international groups which will survive and prosper in the world computer market. CMB with its well-established reputation and clientele in Western Europe is likely to have an important position in one of these groups, and in this event it is probable that De La Rue Bull Machines would be marketing a wider range of equipment than hitherto. Furthermore, the provision of new technical and financial strength for CMB by what ever means, would have favourable repercussions for De La Rue Bull Machines, in the form of new and advanced equipment with shortened delivery dates. Preparations for these eventualities are being made and the recruitment and training programme of this company continues to have high priority.

Shareholders will want to know more when these probable developments become certainties, and also what the full effect of any new arrangements may be. Following our usual procedure, we shall make a special announcement as soon as it is possible to do so.

In the meantime, we have mounted a vigorous sales campaign with special emphasis on the Gamma 10 machine which is ideally suited to the needs of the small, medium, and divisionalized businesses in the United Kingdom. The first of a number of these machines will be installed in a customer's offices in October next.

Factory and Office Buildings

Twenty-five years ago, the Company's offices and factories were, with one small exception, in and around London. The bombing attacks of 1940 destroyed several De La Rue factories and from that time onwards most of the group's expansion has been in the North and Midlands of this country and several countries overseas. Among our latest expansion developments the Gateshead banknote factory, costing just over £1 million, was necessary for technical as well as physical reasons, and the Maidenhead Research and Development buildings were required for the expansion of the development work of the Formica and Thomas De La Rue companies. A new, small office block has been built in Warwick to provide for further expansion by Potterton, and the thermoplastics business has been moved from London to Glenrothes in Scotland.

At this time last year, it was thought that the cost of the building at Gateshead would be financed through a property development company and progress payments were treated accordingly in the accounts, namely as prepayments amounting to just over £200 000. Negotiations are now taking place for a loan from the Board of Trade under the terms of the Local Employment Act, 1960.

Looking ahead—and with more growth in view—the board has been examining the human, economic, and communications problem created by further changes in the location of some of the activities still based in the London area. It is likely that our administrative centres will remain in and around London but, in the longer future, it is unlikely that it will be economically desirable to maintain any large numbers of staff in Central London. Changes that we have made in the past and those we shall make in the future, involve changes of residence and environment for many who work for the companies of the group, but I am glad to say that effective consultation procedures and careful planning enable us to carry out these movements with the minimum of dislocation and hardship. The ultimate aim is to ensure the health and strength of the group as a whole in the conditions of the future, and to

135

achieve this it is impossible to stand still or even stay in the same place for any long period.

The Future

I will not bore shareholders with a recital of the imponderables which must surround any attempt to look into the future, even for so short a time as one year ahead. By recommending an increased dividend after a year in which profits before taxation have remained under pressure, the board has demonstrated its confidence in the immediate future. A recovery in overall profit margins is on the way and will, I hope, be maintained by the elimination of losses in some of our newer ventures. Some of this improvement is expected to occur this year and, with continued progress by our established profit-earners, there is every reason to look for improved results by the group as a whole at the end of the year.

As shareholders know, the board favours links with them, not only through meetings in various parts of the country, but also through a good information service. Our quarterly statements are an important part of our communications links with shareholders but, as my predecessor took care to point out, it could be very misleading if too much significance were attached to the results of any single quarter. This year, in particular, we expect to experience periodical fluctuations, due mostly to the existence of large contracts which require an uneven pattern of deliveries.

As to the more distant future, I can only reaffirm the steady confidence we have always held and demonstrated by our willingness to go ahead with risk-taking projects whenever and wherever we have judged those risks to be acceptable and the possible rewards good enough. I remember a press comment at the end of last year, to the effect that it was 'still far from plain sailing' in the De La Rue Group of companies. I can confirm that this is still so. But I cannot imagine this company retaining its vitality and attraction to shareholders, and to young men and women of this and future generations, unless there is always a challenging element of rough weather in one part of the business or the other. It is so often the hard endeavour applied to the new idea or the new market which, in the end, produces a great business and one of the chief tasks of industrial management is to maintain the urge to keep on trying something newer still.

Staff

I have already said something about the great contribution made by those in the company who devote themselves wholeheartedly to the tasks of ensuring the growth and success of the De La Rue enterprise. I believe that there are still great reserves of power in our company, and that these can be tapped only if due attention is paid to the work of education, training, and management development at all levels. Of one thing I am utterly sure: if we carry on with our forward-looking policies, we shall continue to find those who work in the business ready and willing to accept every challenge with ability and enthusiasm.

I feel certain that shareholders who can come to our annual general meeting at the Café Royal on 29 July will provide me with a message of thanks and encouragement to pass on to the 10 000 men and women who work for the company all over the world.

Exhibit 23.2 The De La Rue Company Limited (C1)

Financial Information 1955–64

Amounts are expressed in thousands of pounds

		1964	1963	1962	1961	1960	1959	1958	1957	1956	1955
Turnover											
Home sales		13 050	9861	8977	8082	8134	6217	5187	5232	4761	4933
Export sales from the United Kingdom		7331	6895	6958	5245	4585	4309	5216	4435	4017	3617
Sales by overseas companies		10 074	7991	5974	5215	4337	3332	3173	1427	1649	—
	A	30 455	24 747	21 909	18 542	17 056	13 858	13 576	11 094	10 427	8550
Group profit before taxation	B	2598	2755	2599	2287	2282	1586	1425	1212	1071	906
Taxation		1026	1421	1494	1185	1141	821	919	700	663	573
Net profit after taxation		1572	1334	1105	1102	1141	765	506	512	408	333
Profit attributable to outside shareholders		523	401	273	341	410	95	91	12	38	—
Profit attributable to The De La Rue Company Limited		1049	933	832	761	731	670	415	500	370	333
Preference dividend		11	11	11	11	11	10	10	10	10	10
Profit attributable to ordinary shareholders	C	1038	922	821	750	720	660	405	490	360	323
Disposal of net profit											
Ordinary dividend		510	468	383	383	306	223	186	186	160	157
Profit retained		528	454	438	367	414	437	219	304	200	166
		1038	922	821	750	720	660	405	490	360	323
Capital employed											
Long-term liabilities		3694	25	—	—	—	—	—	—	—	—
Future taxation		588	724	827	637	670	416	424	535	490	453
Outside shareholders		4943	3862	3460	3280	2717	2121	1345	64	53	4
Preference stockholders		500	500	500	500	500	500	500	500	500	500
		9725	5111	4787	4417	3887	3037	2269	1099	1043	957
Ordinary shareholders—equity interest		11 138	10 548	7302	6894	6253	4750	4027	3448	3144	2976
	D	20 863	15 659	12 089	11 311	10 140	7787	6296	4547	4187	3933
Employment of capital											
Fixed assets		15 799	10 819	9222	7968	5938	4840	3654	2088	2170	2148
Current assets less current liabilities		5064	4840	2867	3343	4202	2947	2642	2459	2017	1785
		20 863	15 659	12 089	11 311	10 140	7787	6296	4547	4187	3933
Profit before taxation as a percentage of average capital employed		13.8%	19.5%	22.2%	21.3%	25.0%	22.5%	26.3%	27.7%	26.4%	24.0%
Profit before taxation as a percentage of turnover (B/A × 100)		8.5%	11.1%	11.9%	12.3%	13.4%	11.4%	10.5%	10.9%	10.3%	10.6%
Profit attributable as a percentage of equity interest (C/D × 100)		9.3%	8.7%	11.2%	10.9%	11.5%	13.9%	10.0%	11.3%	11.4%	10.8%
Ordinary dividend as a percentage of equity interest		7.5%	7.2%	8.6%	9.1%	8.0%	7.8%	8.1%	9.4%	8.8%	9.3%
Earnings for each ordinary share		3s 1d	2s 9d	2s 10d	2s 8d	2s 5½d	2s 7½d	1s 8½d	2s 0½d	1s 5d	1s 3d
Dividend for each ordinary share		1s 6d	1s 4½d	1s 4d	1s 4d	1s 1d	10½d	9½d	9½d	7½d	7½d
Cover for ordinary dividend		2.0	2.0	2.1	2.0	2.3	3.0	2.2	2.6	2.2	2.0

Exhibit 23.3 The De La Rue Company Limited (C1)

London equity prices (adjusted) of:
De La Rue 10s ordinary shares.
Waterlow & Sons (manufacturing stationers and printers) £1 deferred
ordinary shares.
Imperial Chemical Industries Limited £1 ordinary stock.

	De La Rue		Waterlow		ICI	
	Highest	Lowest	Highest	Lowest	Highest	Lowest
1955	11s 8d	7s 6d	27s 6d	16s 6d	27s 1d	16s 10d
1956	9s 1d	6s 7d	27s 3d	19s 7d	21s 11d	15s 10d
1957	11s 3d	7s 2d	31s 6d	23s 6d	20s 6d	15s 5d
1958	15s 6d	9s 2d	31s 0d	22s 0d	25s 1d	15s 7d
1959	34s 4d	13s 5d	56s 6d	23s 0d	41s 4d	21s 7d
1960	48s 4d	28s 0d	55s 0d	37s 6d	50s 6d	35s 2d
1961	42s 5d	25s 10d	54s 0d	45s 0d	54s 7d	35s 10d
1962	37s 4d	30s 4d	80s 0d*	52s 0d*	41s 4d	31s 4d
1963	47s 9d	36s 3d	—	—	50s 10d	35s 10d
1964		37s 9d	—	—		44s 3d
(30 July)						

Capital Changes
March: 1958 capitalization
issue—one ordinary 5s ·
share for each 5s share held,
subsequently consolidated
into 10s shares.
July 1959: 1 for 5 rights
issue at 27s 6d.
August 1960: 1 for 5
capitalization issue.
July 1962: 1 for 1 rights
issue at par.

*To 19 August
takeover.

Capital Changes
May 1958: 1 for 2
capitalization
issue.
Jan. 1961: 1 for 20
rights issue at
55s.
Dec. 1963: 1 for 2
capitalization
issue.
Note: Issues
under profit-
sharing scheme
and conversion
of loan stock
not included.

Exhibit 23.4 **The De La Rue Company Limited (C1)** *DLR Share Indices of De La Rue 10s Ordinary and Economist Extel Indicator (Source: The Economist, 7 November 1964)*

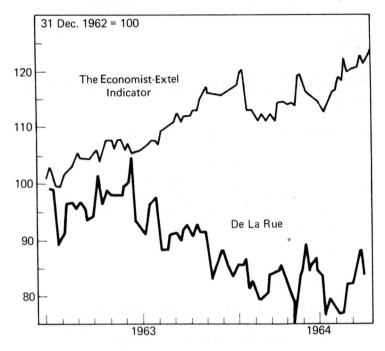

24

The De La Rue Company Limited (C2)*

A year later, Charles Manning received the De La Rue published accounts for the following year's operations (see Exhibits 24.1 and 24.2). He had also kept cuttings from the financial press on all reports about the company. These reports are given as Exhibits 24.4, 24.5, and 25.6.

Question

How much were the reports and comments in the press justified in the next year's operations?

Exhibit 24.1 The De La Rue Company Limited (C2)

The De La Rue Company Limited and Subsidiary Companies
Consolidated Balance Sheet as at 27 March 1965 (£ 000s)

	1965		1964	
CAPITAL EMPLOYED	£	£	£	£
Preference Capital				
3½% Cumulative Preference Stock		500		500
Ordinary Shareholders' Interests				
Ordinary Shares of 10s each	5556		5556	
Capital Reserves	1217		1186	
Undistributed Profits	4876		4396	
		11 649		11 138
Outside Shareholders' Interests		5786		4943
Future Taxation		918		588
Long-Term Liabilities		6126		3694
		24 979		20 863

*Case material of the Management Case Research Programme, Cranfield, Bedford, England, and prepared as a basis for class discussion. This case was made possible through the cooperation of The De La Rue Company Limited. Reproduced by kind permission of the Cranfield School of Management.

EMPLOYMENT OF CAPITAL

Fixed Assets

Land, Buildings, and Plant	14 087		11 701	
Licences, Goodwill, etc.	3534		2428	
Subsidiary Co.s Not Consolidated	946		410	
Trade Investments	1517		1260	
		20 084		15 799

Current Assets

Stocks	7280		5600	
Debtors and Bills	9091		7186	
Cash and Deposits	903		1973	
	17 274		14 759	

Current Liabilities

Creditors and Bills	6359		5605	
Current Tax	522		554	
Overdrafts and Short-Term Loans	4898		3196	
Dividends Unpaid	602		340	
	12 381		9695	
Net Current Assets		4893		5064
		24 979		20 863

Exhibit 24.2 The De La Rue Company Limited (C2)
The De La Rue Company Limited and Subsidiary Companies
Consolidated Profit and Loss Account for the 52 weeks ending 27 March 1965
(£ 000s)

	1965 £	1965 £	1964 £	1964 £
Net Sales		36 422		30 455
Less Cost of Sales		32 864*		27 659*
Trading Profit		3558		2795
Long-Term Interest Paid	268		129	
Short-Term Interest Paid Less Dividends Received	137	405	68	197
Group Profit before Tax		3153		2598
Taxation		1411		1026
Group Profit after Tax		1742		1572
Profit Attributable to Outside Shareholders		726		523
Profit Attributable to The De La Rue Company Limited		1016		1049
Preference Dividend Net		11		11
Profit Attributable to Ordinary Shareholders		1005		1038
Ordinary Dividends (net) (1s 6d per share)		496		510
Profit Retained in the Group		509		528
Balance of Undistributed Profit		4367		3868
Total Undistributed Profit		4876		4396

*Includes operating expenses.

141

Exhibit 24.3 The De La Rue Company Limited (C2)

EXTRACT FROM *THE ECONOMIST* 11 JULY 1964
De La Rue—All Three in Same Direction?

At first sight, the 1964 report and accounts of the De La Rue group might well be taken for that of an American company on account of its design, general layout and the wealth of information which it contains. The report was actually printed by De La Rue's American printing subsidiary, and the venture may perhaps help to take the American printing division out of the red. As the table shows, it was Thomas De La Rue International, covering security printing and, through Security Express, physical security that performed badly last year, with the American losses adding to those made in non-banknote printing in this country. And the chairman, Mr A. G. Norman, forecasts a period of consolidation and possibly some pruning, although not of the fast expanding Security Express group which is now making profits and has set up this week a joint cash and bullion carrying service in Australia.

| | 1962/63 | | | 1963/64 | | |
| | Sales | Pretax profits | Profit margin | Sales | Pretax profits | Profit margin |
	£ 000s		%	£ 000s		%
Formica Intern. Ltd	12 644	1665	13·2	15 433	1847	12·0
Thomas De La Rue Intern. Ltd	7429	845	11·4	9057	644	7·1
Thos. Potterton Ltd	4668	577	12·4	5935	636	10·7
Frigistor Group (European Interests)	6	(13)		30	(32)	
Total	24 747	3074*	12·4	30 455	3095*	10·2

*Before management expenses and debenture interest.

The contribution of Formica rose further with a modest contribution from the Tyboard chipboard acquisition and with the German subsidiary cutting back its losses and set to make a maiden trading profit this year. Competition in this field is keen and Formica has cut many of its prices, but the doubling of chipboard capacity and the ever widening range of decorative laminates produced help to support the chairman's view that the outlook for Formica is 'full of promise'. For the Potterton boiler group rapidly overtaking the security printing side in terms of profits though not turnover, the central heating boom suggests another good year, although ventures into the growing but highly competitive European market, often involving redesign of equipment, may prove profitable only in the longer term.

But for the associated company, De La Rue Bull Machines, in which the group has a £1·37 million stake, the prospect is of a breakeven point being reached in 1965/66, and Mr Norman expects the company to market a much wider range of computer equipment if there is a successful outcome to the present negotiations between its French partner, Compagnie Machines Bull, other French companies, the French government and General Electric of the

United States. This could leave the French company inside one of the six (or less) emerging international computer groups.

But despite Mr Norman's confident forecast, backed by a dividend raised by $1\frac{1}{4}$ points to 15%, the shares are not far above their low for the year and, at 36s are a quarter down on last year's high and over 40% down on the 1962 high. The yield is now 4·2% covered just over twice by earnings up last year thanks to a sharply lower tax ratio. The market is clearly not prepared to put the shares in the supergrowth category as they did in the late 'fifties and early 'sixties, and the past record does not justify it, but profit margins improved steadily throughout the past year. And one year—it could well be 1964/65— the three major divisions are all going to make bigger profits.

Exhibit 24.4 The De La Rue Company Limited (C2)

EXTRACT FROM THE *FINANCIAL TIMES* 30 JULY 1964
De La Rue's Margins

Three points stand out from De La Rue's statement for the first quarter of the current year. First, profit margins have taken a turn for the worse again. In 1963/64 the average was 8·5%, but there was an improvement over the year from 7·3% to $9\frac{3}{4}$%. However, in the 12 weeks to 20 June 1964, margins fell back again to 7·3%. One reason is that there is now debenture interest to pay: but the key factor is the cost of the transfer of banknote production from Leeds to Gateshead. There has also been a loss of banknote export sales. Secondly, Formica International and Thomas Potterton are doing very well indeed and are mostly responsible for the rise of $39\frac{1}{2}$% in home and overseas companies' sales. And thirdly minority interests in the first quarter were nearly double those for the same quarter of 1963/64. This by-product of Formica International's success means that in fact attributable profits for the first quarter are slightly down at £136 000 as compared with £144 000. What is the likely outturn for the whole year?

Given the board's confidence, it seems not unreasonable to suppose that the fall in margins is only temporary and that last year's profits ratio can be held. Thus, if export sales can be maintained at £7·3 million (they were down in the first quarter from £1·9 million to £1 million) and if other sales can be kept up to their $39\frac{1}{2}$% advance so far, then pretax profits could be £3·4 million against £2·6 million. Meanwhile, the 10s Ordinary at 37s 9d yield 3·9%. Cover was 1·4 times on the 1963/64 figures.

Exhibit 24.5 The De La Rue Company Limited (C2)

EXTRACT FROM *THE TIMES* 30 JULY 1964
Good Figures From De La Rue

Profit figures of the De La Rue Company for the first quarter of 1964/65 justify the optimism expressed in the chairman's recent annual review. Total group sales rose from £6 200 000 to £7 million and produced a corresponding increase in group pretax profits from £456 000 to £512 000. Net profits after tax were £76 000 higher at £307 000. Home sales rose from £2 200 000 to £3 300 000 and sales by overseas companies from £2 100 000 to £2 700 000, but export sales from the United Kingdom declined from £1 900 000 to £1 023 000.

At first sight, the reduction in export sales is disappointing. However, the directors explain that the transfer of banknote production from Leeds to Gateshead has temporarily reduced export sales and earnings of Thomas De La Rue International. Thus, the first quarter's figures do not reflect the full improvement expected in the results for the whole year.

As was only to be expected, the chairman made some encouraging remarks at yesterday's annual meeting to the negotiations recently concluded between Compagnie des Machines Bull and the United States General Electric Company. CMB and GE intend to use the existing sales network of De La Rue Bull Machines for the marketing of the GE range of business computers in the United Kingdom market in addition to the whole range of Bull equipment. The ability of the De La Rue Bull Machines to offer a much wider range of computers and data processing equipment to British users would, the chairman pointed out, enable the company to increase more rapidly its growing share of the United Kingdom market.

25

Universe Electronics Limited

Universe Electronics Incorporated was founded in the United States in the 'twenties and was initially concerned with the manufacture of radios and radio components and was in only a small way of business employing some thirty people in all. During the Second World War, it was able to secure large contracts under the Lend-Lease arrangements for the manufacture of radio sets for use in the Army and for other electrical equipment. As a result of its contacts with the government procurement departments, some of its personnel were brought in at the early stages of the development of the atom bomb to deal with certain aspects of monitoring and control of some of the stages of producing fissile material, etc.

The corporation expanded rapidly during the war years and on VE day it employed some 15 000 people in three major plants in the USA. To its monitoring and measuring equipment, it soon was able to add computational equipment as it developed a range of computers for industrial use.

In 1959, the President, Mr John C. Harvey, commissioned a report on the possibilities of expanding into other world markets, particularly in Europe. One of the terms of reference was to look at the implications for the corporation's tax position in the different methods of operating overseas. As a result of this survey, a company was set up in Panama which, in turn, incorporated a subsidiary in Lichtenstein.

The British Company

In view of the likely opening of negotiations for Britain's entry into the Common Market and the advanced state of technology in Britain, it was decided in 1961 that the centre for European operations would be located in the UK, and, accordingly, a small factory was acquired for £150 000 in Bedford. Mr Carlton C. Ward was seconded to manage the European operation and took up residence in England in 1962. Progress was slow at first due to the increasing pressure of competition from fellow American companies and British companies such as Ferranti and Elliott-Automation. This position was not improved by the collapse of negotiations for entry into the Common Market in 1963.

Changes in the Parent Group

In February 1963, the parent company was taken over by a US conglomerate and the top management was replaced by members of the board of this company, Barron, Keogh, and Tighlict. The new board of directors set about reorganizing the new group into a number of semi-autonomous companies, each of which would have a management responsible for the profitability of their own company and profitability targets were to be set for each of the constituent parts. The basic objective of the group is to provide after tax earnings of 15% on the capital employed by each subsidiary company. Progress was being made in this direction when the group, together with other conglomerates, came under considerable fire from academics, government agencies, and investors, and lost the glamour status which they had hitherto enjoyed. The downturn in the US economy provided the stimulus for this by causing sharply lower earnings in the parent group. This, together with the lowered investment status, slashed the share price and caused concern for the liquidity of the group. Active measures were put into effect by the board, among which was a directive to their overseas operations, including that in the UK, to the effect that continued expansion must be financed by retained profits or by using local sources of non-equity finance.

Universe Electronics Limited Long-Range Plan 1968-71

Carlton Ward was replaced by the new management. His successor was an Englishman, Tom Brierly. During the latter part of 1968, he prepared a plan of operations for the next three years with the objective of meeting the parent group's target rate of return (see Exhibit 25.3). In addition to the expansion in fixed assets outlined in that plan, he had come to the conclusion that he would need to provide considerable business computing facilities to handle the company's increased data processing requirements, and to provide for more sophisticated management control. In view of the heavy investment (£120 000) that this would require, he was actively considering how this should be financed. Because of the credit squeeze which had been in effect for some four years and which had been intensified recently, the bank was pressing for some reduction in the bank overdraft, but he felt that because a high proportion of the company's products (40%) was exported that, if he pressed hard enough, he could probably finance this through additional bank borrowing, although it would not be easy to arrange; it would, in any case, cost getting on for 10% per annum. He ruled out the use of hire purchase, since current effective rates of interest charged were getting on for 20% and the company would still have to provide part of the cost in cash because of government restrictions.

The Leasing Proposal

At a Christmas party held at a friend's house at the end of 1968, Brierly met an executive of Plant Leasing Facilities Limited, Mr D. E. Tilling. During the course of the party, he had been telling him of his difficulties in financing the purchase of the equipment that he needed and Tilling suggested that they meet early in the new year so that he could provide him with details of their leasing facilities.

This meeting took place on 5 January 1969, and, after further discussions with the suppliers of the equipment Vacco Limited, a detailed schedule of the equipment and costs was submitted to Plant Leasing on 13 January.

Because of the high rate of obsolescence of computers, it was agreed that the leasing period would not be for more than six years, although, if Universe continued to use the equipment after that period, they would only have to pay a nominal rental of £1000 per year. Insurance and all other ownership costs would be borne by Universe in the normal way and, to safeguard the operating efficiency of the equipment, Universe would have to enter into a full maintenance contract with the supplier the benefits of which would be assignable to Plant Leasing. If Universe owned the equipment, some of the servicing would be carried out by its own technical staff and it would be able to save some £2000 per year of the cost of full maintenance.

Brierly was most concerned to see that the forecast expansion of activities was not inhibited by the use of funds to provide the computer. The restriction of bank-lending and cutting back by the parent

147

company had already led to a slow drop in expansion in 1968 and, if the targets that he was setting were to be reached, implimentation of the plan should begin at once. He recognized that one of his major headaches over the next three years would be the control of trade credit extended to customers. While the long-range plan had been based upon keeping to a two month average collection period, he had become aware recently that it was becoming more difficult to collect outstanding amounts and, if the collection was to lengthen significantly, this would effect the volume of funds that he would require. Some of this might be offset by lengthening the payment period to creditors, but the decline in the liquidity ratios since 1966 shown by the long-range plan might make this difficult.

The possibility of raising additional long-term funds had been considered and he had been given to understand by the parent company that this might be acceptable. There were, however, two problems. First, the buildings, etc., were already mortgaged and, if effective use of property values was to be made in financing, it would be prudent to first pay off this liability. Second, there was the time factor. A decision on the new computing equipment was needed in the next few days if they were to maintain the timetable for installation, but the arranging of new long-term borrowing would take some time, and, in any case, it was felt that interest rates were historically too high (about 10%) to enter into major long-term commitments.

Exhibit 25.1 Universe Electronics Limited

Profit and Loss Accounts for the Years to 31 December

	1966 £	1967 £	1968 £
Sales	832 740	1 193 400	1 362 410
Operating Profit (after depreciation: 1966 £20 913; 1967 £27 964; 1968 £32 682)	51 342	62 964	77 420
Less Mortgage Interest	4000	4000	4000
Profit before Tax	47 342	58 964	73 420
Corporation Tax	18 100	24 110	29 310
Profit after Tax	29 242	34 854	44 110
Loss on Plant Scrapped	4125	—	—
	25 117	34 854	44 110
Retained Profit Brought Forward	40 181	59 423	79 277

	1966	1967	1968
Available for Distribution	65 298	94 277	123 387
Dividends (Net 1966; gross 1967 and 1968)	5875	15 000	20 000
	59 423	79 277	103 387

Exhibit 25.2 Universe Electronics Limited

Balance Sheets as at 31 December:

	1966	1967	1968
	£	£	£
Fixed Assets			
Buildings	150 000	150 000	150 000
Plant and Equipment at Cost	139 420	186 430	217 880
Less Depreciation	46 890	74 854	107 536
	92 530	111 576	110 344
	242 530	261 576	260 344
Current Assets			
Stocks and WIP	117 540	169 800	256 210
Debtors and Prepayments	141 100	199 080	254 100
Cash in Hand	3640	5120	4960
	262 280	374 000	515 270
	504 810	635 576	775 614
Less *Current Liabilities*			
Bank Overdraft	47 126	115 174	145 720
Creditors	59 760	91 480	164 310
Accrued Expenses	6931	7435	8777
Tax Due	13 470	18 100	24 110
	127 287	232 189	342 917
Net Assets	£377 523	£403 387	£432 697
Financed as follows			
Share Capital £1 Ordinary Shares	250 000	250 000	250 000
Retained Profit	59 423	79 277	103 387
	309 423	329 277	353 387
8% Mortgage (Secured on Property)	50 000	50 000	50 000
Future Tax	18 100	24 110	29 310
	£377 523	£403 387	£432 697

Exhibit 25.3 Universe Electronics Limited
Extract from Financial Targets for the Three Year Period 1969/71

	1969	1970	1971
	£	£	£
Sales	1 600 000	2 000 000	2 750 000
After Tax Profits	63 000	94 000	137 000
Dividends	20 000	20 000	20 000
Increase in Retained Profits	43 000	74 000	117 000
Assets			
Buildings	150 000	200 000	200 000
Plant (Cost)	300 000	370 000	460 000
Plant (Depreciation)	150 000	205 500	274 500
Stocks and WIP	350 000	450 000	550 000
Debtors, etc.	270 000	333 000	460 000
Liabilities			
Creditors	210 000	230 000	300 000
Accrued Liabilities	9000	10 000	11 000

Exhibit 25.4 Universe Electronics Limited

PLANT LEASING FACILITIES LIMITED

92 Ledminster Street,
LONDON EC4.

Ref. JBB/DET

23 February 1969

T. Brierly Esq,
Managing Director,
Universe Electronics Limited,
Bowminster Way,
BEDFORD.

Dear Mr Brierly,

PROPOSED COMPUTER LEASE

Following our discussions of your requirements during our visit to your plant on Friday last, we have now been able to draw up proposals for the leasing to yourselves of the Vacco 7240 computer and peripheral equipment detailed in your letter of 13 January 1969.

On the basis of the cost quoted to you by Vacco Limited of £120 000 for the complete installation, we would be prepared to purchase the equipment from Vacco Limited and lease it to yourselves on the basis of a rental of £26 000 per annum for a minimum period of six years. If the lease continues after the six year period, the rental will be reduced to £1000 per annum.

The terms of the lease will include provisions for your entering into an agreement with Vacco for the servicing of the installation in accordance with their quotation to yourselves of 17 January 1969. This agreement will contain provision for the assignment to ourselves of the benefits of this agreement.

150

In view of the present economic uncertainties, the above offer will remain open to you for thirty days, but we reserve the right to alter the terms after that time should circumstances so require. Upon receipt of your agreement to the terms we will at once write to Vacco enclosing a firm order for the equipment in accordance with the terms quoted, so that the delivery date which you are concerned about can be met.

Yours sincerely,

D. E. Tilling,
London Regional Manager,
Plant Leasing Facilities Limited

26

The Nulite Electrical Company Limited*

The Nulite Electrical Company Limited was formed in 1947 by Gordon Smith and Peter Standing. When they were demobilized from the Forces, they jointly invested £500 of their gratuities to start an electrical business. Their first products consisted of standard and other decorative lamps, mainly for domestic use, but by 1949 the lamps were also used in commercial offices.

The company prospered and by the late 'fifties the product range consisted of decorative lamps, chime bells, and electric food mixers.

The company's factory was on the western outskirts of London. During the fifteen years from 1949, the company had become used to having to change and sometimes enlarge their production premises. This was generally due to the increasing demand for the company's products.

In September 1966, the company, for the first time, planned its activities for the future. The initial plan only covered the year 1967 and, after careful assessment of market factors and available economic data, the 1967 plan was transformed into a budget (Exhibit 26.1). The budget approach was decided upon after Smith and Standing, still the only shareholding directors (although not the only shareholders), were worried about the cash difficulties from which the company suffered. They could not understand why they were not able to get rid of the company's overdraft, which the bank only granted on the personal guarantee of Smith and Standing.

---

*This case is reproduced by kind permission of Eric A. Ward, FCWA, AMBIM. The case study concerns a practical business situation, but the company and the individuals concerned have been given fictitious names. Figures used have been adjusted so that no relationship to any existing company can be established.

To add to their concern, they found that expansion beyond the 1967 budget figures could only take place if additional buildings could be made available. As there was no further room on the present site, the company would have to face, if it wanted to expand, either operating from two locations or a move to a site big enough to allow it to operate under one roof, not only in 1968, but in the foreseeable future beyond that. In the London area, proposals for new factory buildings with a floor area above 3000 square feet need an Industrial Development Certificate which the company would have little chance of obtaining.

On top of these headaches, early in 1967, when the 1966 results became available (Exhibits 26.2 and 26.3), it was found that the 1966 profit was low. It was only 12·5% on the shareholder's funds, and that was before Corporation Tax was deducted, quite apart from income tax which the shareholders would have to pay on any dividend declared.

When Gordon Smith had a drink at his local one evening soon after the 1966 profit was ascertained, he met Charles Lufkins who was the local manager of a building society. Smith said, 'We only made 12·5% profit on the investment last year; I am very disappointed, but I suppose if I compare it with the miserable 4·5% your society pays, I ought to be well satisfied.'

'Money earns more in a Building Society,' retorted Lufkins, and explained that, after deducting 40% Corporation Tax and then 8s 3d in the £ for income tax on dividends, an investment in Nulite is worth to the shareholder only 4·41%.

'It seems all wrong,' said Smith, 'that with so much money locked up in the company, we earn so little. You have really given me something to think about.'

It seemed to Gordon Smith that, although the company achieved a record of sales, in future they would be still shorter of cash. Also, they were running out of space with, so he downheartedly surmised, neither site nor money to get one. On top of all that, profits were unsatisfactory. When he told Standing about this unsatisfactory situation, Standing said 'Our products are very good, the market readily accepts them and some of our new products are already at the testing stage—and yet, your analysis of the situation seems to be correct. I must think about these problems.'

At lunchtime, Raymond Cliff, a director of one of Nulite's suppliers who had long ago arranged a lunch for that day with Smith

153

and Standing, had to listen to the depressed analysis of the Nulite situation.

'I have had similar problems some years ago and ever since we have gone from strength to strength,' he said to the Nulite directors. 'John Nobes is a consultant well experienced in company growth problems. He may be able to advise you.'

Smith and Standing decided to call Nobes in to assist. After acquainting him with the history and current situation of the business, it was decided that a six year plan should be prepared for the years 1968–73.

Bearing in mind the life of the existing products and the marketing of new ones, a plan was established which showed 20% compound growth in five of the six years (Exhibit 26.4).

Cost factors were then carefully assessed, particular attention being paid to the movement in the relatively fixed overhead expenses. The costs and profit projection revealed substantial profit potential (Exhibit 26.5).

The provision of necessary buildings and other fixed assets was included in a separate tabulation (Exhibit 26.6).

Finally, a balance sheet was projected for the current year and for each year of the plan (Exhibit 26.7).

Smith and Standing liked the sales and profit figures, and they were particularly pleased with the implication in the fixed assets projection (Exhibit 26.6) that they would be working only in modern buildings and with up to date plant.

Having personally guaranteed the bank overdraft, they very much wished this to be eliminated, but the balance sheet projection (Exhibit 26.7) showed the overdraft to be increasing. The consultant explained to them that if quick assets and current liabilities were in a relationship of 1 : 1 there would be nothing to worry about.

Further examination of the 1966 actual and 1967–73 projected figures showed that current liabilities exceeded quick assets in every year of the projection.

The consultant then extracted the quick assets shortages to the desired 1 : 1 ratio (Exhibit 26.8).

Smith and Standing wanted the existing shareholders to benefit from the future, if this was at all possible. As long as a moderately rising dividend could be paid on existing equity capital, the shareholders were not likely to be very troublesome in clamouring for more.

They did not want to plan for long-term debt, but they were prepared to use some debt if no other solution could be found or if their plan of expansion suffered some setback. But they did not view long-term debt kindly.

The consultant mentioned that government financial aid was available to encourage companies to move into development areas. The accountant of Nulite therefore obtained data about the assistance and produced a tabulation (Exhibit 26.9) of available investment grants. Grants for plant and machinery, which were available on a lower scale in areas other than development districts, had already been taken into account in Exhibits 26.6 and 26.7. A list of parts of the country designated as development areas was also made available (Exhibit 26.10).

The amount of grants which could apparently be obtained were so considerable that it was decided to examine the possibility of a move to a development district. Further information on area sales (Exhibit 26.11), personnel requirements (Exhibit 26.12), rates of pay (Exhibit 26.13), and other special cost factors was produced (Exhibit 26.14).

Smith and Standing were very pleased to see that the quick position (Exhibit 26.15a) following a move was so much better. They became really enthusiastic about the move when they saw that the assets value of their investment would be multiplied by more than eight (Exhibit 26.16) and nobody but the existing shareholders would share in the increased value.

Exhibit 26.1 The Nulite Electrical Company Limited
Extract from Budget for 1967 (All figures in £ 000s)

Sales		1080
Costs		
Direct Labour	86	
Direct Materials	475	
Overheads	424	
	——	
		985
Profit		95

Exhibit 26.2 The Nulite Electrical Company Limited
Profit and Loss Account

Period: 1 January 1966 to 31 December 1966 (All figures in £ 000s)

Direct Labour Costs	80		Sales	1000
Direct Material Costs	440			
Factory Overheads	220			
Total Factory Cost		740		
Factory Profit		260		
		1000		1000
Administration Overhead		90	Factory Profit	260
Selling and Distribution Overhead		105		
Net Profit (Subject to Tax)		65		
		260		260
Tax		26	Net Profit	65
Proposed Dividend (Gross)		15		
General Reserve		5		
Profit and Loss Account		19		
		65		65

Exhibit 26.3 The Nulite Electrical Company Limited
Balance Sheet as at 31 December 1966 (All figures in £ 000s)

Liabilities			Assets	At cost	Depr.	
Authorized and Issued			Freehold Property	96	—	96
Share Capital		250	Plant and			
Capital Reserve		60	Machinery	350	125	225
General Reserve	40		Motor Vehicles	40	25	15
Profit and Loss Account	170	210	Furniture	12	2	10
Total Shareholders' Funds		520	*Total Fixed Assets*			346
Future Tax		26				
Trade Creditors	130					
Tax due 1.1.67	35					
Dividend (Proposed)	15		Stock and WIP			260
Overdraft	100		Debtors			220
Total Current Liabilities		280	*Total Current Assets*			480
		826				826

156

$$\frac{\text{Sales}}{\text{Shareholders' Funds}} = £\frac{1\ 000\ 000}{520\ 000} = 1.93$$ (Shareholders' funds turned over 1·93 times)

$$\frac{\text{Profit before tax}}{\text{Shareholders' Funds}} = £\frac{65\ 000}{520\ 000} = 12.5\%$$ (Return on Shareholders' Investment 12·5%)

$$\frac{\text{Current assets}}{\text{Current Liabilities}} = £\frac{480\ 000}{280\ 000} = 1.71$$ (Current assets £1 14s 2d for each £ of current liabilities)

$$\frac{\text{Quick assets}}{\text{Current Liabilities}} = £\frac{220\ 000}{280\ 000} = 0.79$$ (15/10 quickly available for each £ of current liabilities)

$$\frac{\text{Debtors}}{\text{Sales}} = £\frac{220\ 000}{1\ 000\ 000} = 22\%$$ (Debtors are 2·64 months of average sales)

$$\frac{\text{Stock and WIP}}{\text{Sales}} = £\frac{260\ 000}{1\ 000\ 000} = 26\%$$ (Inventory investment 3·12 months of average sales. Remember that inventory valuation is on cost, not sales figures)

Exhibit 26.4 The Nulite Electrical Company Limited

7 Year Long-Term Projection—Sales and Production

Budget	£ 000s	Increase over
1967		previous year
6 *Year Plan*	1080	8%
1968	1300	20%
1969	1560	20%
1970	1870	20%
1971	2240	20%
1972	2690	20%
1973	3000	12%

Exhibit 26.5 The Nulite Electrical Company Limited

7 Year Long-Term Projection—Costs and Profits (All figures in £ 000s)

	Actual	Budget			6 Year Plan			
	1966	1967	1968	1969	1970	1971	1972	1973
Direct Labour Cost	80	86	104	125	150	179	215	240
Direct Material Cost	440	475	572	686	823	986	1184	1320
Overheads								
Directly Variable	115	124	150	179	215	259	309	345
Relatively Fixed	300	320	350	350	430	430	575	575
	935	1005	1176	1340	1618	1854	2283	2480
Sales	1000	1080	1300	1560	1870	2240	2690	3000
Profit	65	75	124	220	252	386	407	520

157

Exhibit 26.6 The Nulite Electrical Company Limited

7 Year Long-Term Projection—Fixed Assets (All figures in £ 000s)

	Actual	Budget			6 Year Plan			
	1966	1967	1968	1969	1970	1971	1972	1973
As at 1 January		346	370	460	520	620	740	900
Additions: Buildings		75	120	120	120	120	145	—
*Additions: Plant and Machinery		12	85	100	90	125	150	160
Total before Year's Depreciation		433	575	680	730	865	1035	1060
Year's Depreciation		58	67	79	91	109	131	146
		375	508	601	639	756	904	914
Sale: Old Buildings		—	40	72	—	—	—	—
Sale: Old Plant and Machinery		5	8	9	19	16	4	4
As at 31 December	346	370	460	520	620	740	900	910

*Net figures after deduction of investment grants at:
25% of plant and machinery 1967 and 1968 purchases;
20% of plant and machinery 1969 and beyond purchases (assumed).

Exhibit 26.7 The Nulite Electrical Company Limited

7 Year Long-Term Projection—Balance Sheet (All figures in £ 000s)

	Actual	Budget			6 Year Plan			
	1966	1967	1968	1969	1970	1971	1972	1973
ASSETS								
Fixed Assets, Net	346	370	460	520	620	740	900	910
Stock and WIP	260	280	335	400	480	570	685	760
Debtors	220	240	285	345	410	495	595	660
Cash	—	—	—	—	—	—	—	—
	826	890	1080	1265	1510	1805	2180	2330
LIABILITIES								
Shareholders' Funds	520	547	599	701	817	1004	1193	1435
Future Tax	26	30	50	88	101	154	163	208
Trade Creditors	130	140	170	205	245	295	350	390
Tax due, 1 January next	35	26	30	50	88	101	154	163
Dividend (proposed)	15	18	22	30	35	45	55	70
Overdraft	100	129	209	191	224	206	265	64
	826	890	1080	1265	1510	1805	2180	2330

Exhibit 26.8 The Nulite Electrical Company Limited
Liquid Position, Quick Assets: Current Liabilities = A Desirable Relationship of 1:1

Quick Assets Shortage to 1:1 Ratio (Based on Exhibit 26.7 Projection)

	Quick Assets £ 000s	Current Liabilities £ 000s	Shortage £ 000s
1966 Actual	220	280	60
1967 Budget	240	313	73
6 Year Plan:			
1968	285	431	146
1969	345	476	131
1970	410	592	182
1971	495	647	152
1972	595	824	229
1973	660	687	27

Exhibit 26.9 The Nulite Electrical Company Limited
Investment Grants

National
Buildings Nil
Plant and Machinery: 25% to 31.12.68
Assumed reverting to 20% from 1969

Amount of Grant
Plant and Machinery Expenditure: 1967/68 = £129 000; 25% = £32 000
1969/73 = £781 000; 20% = £156 000

(Approximate Total) £188 000

Development District
Buildings: 25%
Plant and Machinery: 45% to 31.12.68
Assumed reverting to 40% from 1969

Amount of Grant
Building Expenditure: 1967/68 = £195 000; 25% = £49 000
1969/73 = £505 000; 25% = £126 000
Plant and Machinery Expenditure: 1967/68 = £129 000; 45% = £58 000
1969/73 = £781 000; 40% = £312 000

£545 000

National	£188 000
Development Area	£545 000
Extra Benefit to Development Area	£357 000

Note: Capital allowances will be restricted to amount of capital expenditure less grants. Discounted cash flow techniques may be used to calculate effect of timing.

Exhibit 26.10 The Nulite Electrical Company Limited
List of Development Areas

The areas are defined by reference to Ministry of Labour Employment Exchange areas or groups of such areas. The Board of Trade Regional Office responsible for each development area is indicated below. All towns in the areas are not necessarily mentioned individually.

Scottish Development Area (Board of Trade Office for Scotland)
All Scotland except the Edinburgh, Leith, and Portobello Employment Exchange areas.

Northern Development Area (Board of Trade Northern Regional Office)
The Ministry of Labour Northern Region plus the Furness Peninsula and Grange-over-Sands suboffice area. It comprises the following Ministry of Employment and Productivity Employment Exchange areas:

Alnwick
Amble
Appleby
Ashington
Aspatria
Barnard Castle Group
　(Barnard Castle and Middleton-in-
　Teesdale)
Barrow-in-Furness Group
　(Barrow-in-Furness and
　Dalton-in-Furness)*
Bedlington
Berwick upon Tweed
Bishop Auckland Group
　(Bishop Auckland, Evenwood,
　Crook, Shildon)
Blyth
Carlisle Group
　(Brampton and Carlisle)
Chester-le-Street Group
　(Birtley, Chester-le-Street and
　Houghton-le-Spring)
Consett
Darlington Group
　(Aycliffe and Darlington)
Durham
Grange-over-Sands*
Guisborough
Haltwhistle

Haswell
Helmsley
Hexham
Kendal
Keswick
Loftus
Malton
Millom
Morpeth
Northallerton
Penrith
Peterlee
Pickering
Prudhoe
Richmond
Saltburn
Scarborough
Seaham
Seaton Delaval
Spennymoor
Stanley Group
　(Lanchester and Stanley)
Stokesley
Sunderland Group
　(Pallion, Southwick, Sunderland,
　and Washington)
Tees-side Group
　(Billingham, Middlesbrough,
　Redcar, South Bank and

*Any inquiries about these particular localities should be addressed to the Board of Trade North-Western Regional Office in Manchester.

Hartlepool Group
(Hartlepool and West Hartlepool)
Tyneside Group
(Blaydon, East Boldon, Elswick
Felling, Gateshead, Jarrow and
Hebburn, Newburn, Newcastle
upon Tyne, North Shields, South
Shields, Walker, Wallsend, West
Moor, and Whitley Bay)
Ulverston*
Whitby

Stockton, and Thornaby)
Thirsk
Whitehaven Group
(Cleator Moor and
Whitehaven)
Wigton
Windermere
Wingate
Workington Group
(Cockermouth, Maryport, and
Workington)

Merseyside Development Area (Board of Trade North-Western Regional Office)
The Employment Exchange areas in this development area are:

Birkenhead Group
(Bebington, Birkenhead and
Wallasey)
Ellesmere Port
Hoylake
Liverpool Group
(Bootle, Crosby, Garston, Kirkby,
Liverpool, Old Swan, Regent Road
[Liverpool], and Walton)

Neston
Prescot
Runcorn
St Helens
Widnes

(Skelmersdale New Town and Winsford will qualify for the benefits available within the Merseyside development area)

Welsh Development Area (Board of Trade Office for Wales)
The whole of Wales and Monmouthshire, except the following employment exchange areas:
1. South-East Wales—Abergavenny–Cardiff Group (Barry, Bute Docks, Cardiff, Llantwit Major, Penarth), the Newport Group (Newport and Newport Docks), Chepstow, Cwmbran and the Monmouth suboffice area.
2. North Wales—the Shotton Group (Buckley, Flint, Holywell, Mold, and Shotton), Rhyl, Colwyn Bay, and Llandudno.

South-Western Development Area (Board of Trade South-Western Regional Office)
The employment exchange areas in the south-western development area are:

Barnstaple
Bideford
Bodmin
Bude
Camelford
Falmouth
Helston

Mevagissey
Newquay Group
(Newquay and Perranporth)
Penzance Group
(Penzance, St Ives, St Just-in-
Penwith, and St Mary's—Isle of
Scilly)

Ilfracombe
Launceston
Liskeard Group
  (Liskeard and Looe)

Redruth Group
  (Camborne, Hayle, and Redruth)
St Austell
Truro
Wadebridge

Exhibit 26.11 The Nulite Electrical Company Limited
Sales Analysed to Areas
Sales of the Company's Products were as follows (in 1966)

	£
Export: Common Market Countries (mostly Germany and Benelux)	60 000
Export: European Free Trade Area	80 000
Export: Outside Europe	40 000
	180 000
United Kingdom	820 000
	£1 000 000

UK sales were further analysed as follows:

	£
London, Home Counties, and South-East	250 000
Lancashire, Yorkshire, and North (including Scotland)	170 000
West of England and Wales	100 000
Midlands and Rest of UK	300 000
	£820 000

Exhibit 26.12 The Nulite Electrical Company Limited
Personnel Requirements

1968 output plan requires:

	Male	Female	Total
Age 18 or over	205	90	
Below age 18	25	15	
	230	105	335

If the company decides to move to a development area, it is thought that no more than approximately 30 key personnel (mostly adult males) will be prepared to move with the company. The necessary training programme for the direct production workers who are to be engaged is estimated as follows:

	Training Period	
	Off job	On job
Machine Shop Workers (approx. 70)	9 weeks	3 weeks
Assembly Shop Workers (approx. 60)	6 weeks	2 weeks
Other Workers	—	3 weeks

Financial training assistance is available from the Ministry of Employment and Productivity (if the firm moves to a development area) as follows:
Off job training free, but firm may have to pay employee's wages while undergoing training.
On job training, financial grants as follows:

	Male	Female
Age 18 or over	£5 0s 0d weekly	£3 10s 0d weekly
Below age 18	£2 10s 0d weekly	£2 0s 0d weekly

Half the tuition fees for approved training in managerial, supervisory, or technical subjects may also be refunded.

Exhibit 26.13 The Nulite Electrical Company Limited

Development Areas: Rates of Pay

These have been found to be, on average, 1s 3d in the £ below those payable at the company's present location. Therefore:

If London Index	100
Development Area Index	$93\frac{3}{4}$

Exhibit 26.14 The Nulite Electrical Company Limited

Special Costs Factor: Factory Overheads and Extra Costs

1. The 1966 profit and loss account (Exhibit 26.2) includes under 'factory overheads' the following costs incurred in that year:

	£
Material Handling Costs	42 000
Plant Maintenance Costs	9000
Building Maintenance Costs	12 000
Heating Costs	6000

It is estimated that in modern premises these costs would have been as follows:

	£
Material Handling Costs	25 000
Plant Maintenance Costs	9000
Building Maintenance Costs	5000
Heating Costs	4000

2. Extra costs will be incurred if located in a development area. On a 1966 basis these are estimated as:

	Extra cost per annum £
Travelling (mainly by Directors and Executives)	4000
Telephone	1000

163

Exhibit 26.15a The Nulite Electrical Company Limited
Liquid Position If Moved to Development Area

	1	2	3	4
	Shortage*	Extra value of development area grant (cumulative)†	1:1 Ratio shortage*	1:1 Ratio surplus*
	£ 000s	£ 000s	£ 000s	£ 000s
1968	146	21	125	
1969	131	70	61	
1970	182	120	62	
1971	152	166		14
1972	229	219	10	
1973	27	284		257

*See Exhibit 26.8.
†This column is based on Exhibit 26.15d.

Exhibit 26.15b The Nulite Electrical Company Limited
Cash Movements: Buildings

Taxation: 40% Corporation Tax. Assume: 15% initial allowance, 2% annual allowance.

1. *In a Non-Development Area*

Year	Cash Out	Cash In in respect of buildings built in year:						Total
		1967	1968	1969	1970	1971	1972	
	£	£	£	£	£	£	£	£
1968	120 000	5100						5100
1969	120 000	600	8160					8760
1970	120 000	600	960	8160				9720
1971	120 000	600	960	960	8160			10 680
1972	145 000	600	960	960	960	8160		11 640
1973	—	600	960	960	960	960	9860	14 300

2. *In a Development Area*

Year	Cash Out	Cash In in respect of buildings built in year:						Total
		1967	1968	1969	1970	1971	1972	
	£	£	£	£	£	£	£	£
1968	120 000	18 750 / 3825						} 22 575
1969	120 000	450	30 000 / 6120					} 36 570
1970	120 000	450	720	30 000 / 6120				} 37 290
1971	120 000	450	720	720	30 000 / 6120			} 38 010
1972	145 000	450	720	720	720	30 000 / 6120		} 38 730
1973	—	450	720	720	720	720	36 250 / 1395	} 46 975

Exhibit 26.15c The Nulite Electrical Company Limited
Cash Movement: Plant

Taxation: 40% Corporation Tax, assume 12·5% annual allowance (straight line).

1. *In a Non-Development Area*

Year	Cash Out	Cash In in respect of plant bought in year:						Total
		1967	**1968**	**1969**	**1970**	**1971**	**1972**	
	£	£	£	£	£	£	£	£
1968	113 333	4000						4600
		600						
1969	125 000		28 333					33 183
		600	4250					
1970	112 500			25 000				34 850
		600	4250	5000				
1971	156 250				22 500			36 850
		600	4250	5000	4500			
1972	187 500					31 250		51 850
		600	4250	5000	4500	6250		
1973	200 000						37 500	58 100
		600	4250	5000	4500	6250		

2. *In a Development Area*

Year	Cash Out	Cash In in respect of plant bought in year:						Total
		1967	**1968**	**1969**	**1970**	**1971**	**1972**	
	£	£	£	£	£	£	£	£
1968	113 333	7200						7640
		440						
1969	125 000		51 000					54 557
		440	3117					
1970	112 500			50 000				57 307
		440	3117	3750				
1971	156 250				45 000			55 682
		440	3117	3750	3375			
1972	187 500					62 500		77 870
		440	3117	3750	3375	4688		
1973	200 000						75 000	90 370
		440	3117	3750	3375	4688		

Exhibit 26.15d The Nulite Electrical Company Limited
Summary of Cash In*

Year	Non-development area	Development area	Difference	Cumulative difference
	£	£	£	£
1968	9700	30 215	20 515	20 515
1969	41 943	91 127	49 184	69 699
1970	44 570	94 597	50 027	119 726
1971	47 530	93 692	46 162	165 888
1972	63 490	116 600	53 110	218 998
1973	72 400	137 345	64 945	283 943

*This summary is based on Exhibits 26.15b and 26.15c.

Exhibit 26.16   The Nulite Electrical Company Limited

Value of Company

Assuming that company valued at 10 times profit/earnings after Corporation Tax. (Based on average of 3 years' earnings.) (Dividend expectations excellent in view of excellent quick position from 1973—see Exhibit 26.15.)

As at end of	Profit after Corporation Tax £ 000s	3 Year average £ 000s	Value of Company (nearest £100 000)
1966	39	32	£300 000
1967	45	38	£400 000
1968	74	53	£500 000
1969	132	84	£800 000
1970	151	119	£1 200 000
1971	232	172	£1 700 000
1972	244	209	£2 100 000
1973	312	263	£2 600 000

27

Pearson Group Limited

The Pearson Group is the successor company to a business started up in the eighteen-nineties. Originally based upon shipbuilding and the armaments industries, it had diversified considerably in the nineteen-thirties when its traditional business virtually collapsed. Since the Second World War, its business has been oriented to the provision of plant and equipment for the newer industries of plastics and chemicals, and the construction of oil refineries. Its other engineering activities include paper-making and other coating plant, and machine tools, particularly for the motor industry.

Although the results have tended to fluctuate to some extent with the fortunes of the industries which it serves, Pearsons has built up a record of slowly increasing profits. Much of the growth has been financed by the retention of earnings, but resort has been made from time to time to rights issues, these include a 3 for 5 rights issue in 1964, a 1 for 4 in 1965, and a 1 for 1 in 1967.

At the board meeting held in the first week of March 1969, the board passed a resolution to increase the interim dividend for the year to 30 June 1969 from 13% to 15% and that, subject to the approval of the Treasury (if this was required at that time), the final would be increased to 20% making 35% for the year. Early in November 1969, the board issued a statement to the effect that current trading was very satisfactory and the company was confident of a further material improvement in the earnings for the year to 30 June 1970.

Shortly after this meeting, Mr Maltby, the finance director of the group, was considering the capital budget which had been prepared by his staff for the following year. The group's capital expenditure had for some years been subject to the control of a 'capital expenditure committee' whose function had been to receive proposals from line and other managers for projected major expansion projects at least one year in advance of any expenditure being required. If approved in principle at this stage, a detailed assessment of the capital expenditure required and the likely return was then submitted to the committee for final approval.

Other capital expenditure was controlled by the committee in total sums, i.e., for replacements and cost-saving machinery within £5000 for each machine and £25 000 in total for each operating division; for non-revenue producing investments, etc., divisional managers had the authority to spend up to £100 per item, with a maximum of £15 000 in any year. Any expenditure above these limits required the sanction of the capital expenditure committee.

The schedule of new investment for the year to June 1971 showed John Maltby that the likely total expenditure requirements for that year would be of the order of £4 million made up as follows:

	£	Estimated after tax return
Mechanization of Materials Stores	120 000	15%
Purchase of Computer Installation and Ancillary Equipment (this will commit £30 000 a year for the next five years for software)	134 000	9%
Erection of New Building for Extension to Press Shop and the Purchase of Additional Machinery	576 000	12%
Purchase of Office Building on Contiguous Site	666 500	7%
Replacement to Power House 'A' Site	482 000	10%
Launch New Range of Office Equipment (Development Authorized 1966):		
Plant and Equipment	823 000 ⎱	
Work in Progress	37 000 ⎰ 10–15%	
Initial Marketing Costs	85 000	
Modernize London Headquarters	120 000	4%
Replacement Plant	280 000	9%
Purchase of Computer Controlled Machines	423 000	10%
Provision of New Sportsfield and Pavilion	90 000	—
Refitting Canteen Kitchens	35 000	5%
Replacement of Typewriters by New Electrics	40 000	6%
Reconstruction of Loading Facilities to Accommodate New Heavy Plant Deliveries	120 000	7%
	£4 031 500	

Maltby was most concerned about the total expenditure that the committee was being asked to approve. As finance director, he was

aware that the bank, as a result of pressure from the Chancellor of
the Exchequer, was pressing for the company to reduce its overdraft,
and at the same time the current expansion of the existing activities
of the business would make some demands upon the cash resources
during the next year.

Even after taking into account the cash flows that would be
generated within the group in that year, expenditure at the current
levels would entail some recourse to outside sources of finance. He
had therefore been considering some of the alternatives that were
available. These included:

1. A further debenture issue. This would require a special resolution
   to be passed at the forthcoming annual general meeting to increase
   the directors' borrowing powers. He looked at the prices of some
   recent issues which included the following:

Company	Issue	Issue price £	Current price £
Dixon (P)	9½% Convertible Loan 1981–85 (£25 paid)	99	34
J. Lewis Props.	10% Debenture Stock 1991–96 (£25 paid)	98½	27
Southend Water	10% Redeemable Stock 1992–94	96	102
United Drapery	10½% Debenture Stock 1989–94 (£25 paid)	100	27¼

2. A further issue of preference shares. The company's financial
   advisers had advised against this in view of the few issues that
   there had been since the 1965 Finance Act. Maltby felt, however,
   that they should be considered since, in his view, they would
   enable the company to avoid the dilution aspect of a rights issue
   and at the same time not add to the debt burden which the loan
   alternative would entail. The returns offered to investors by some
   existing issues were as follows:

Company	Issue	Price	Dividend yield
Delta Metal	£1 4½% Preference	9s 7½d	9·7
Cadbury Schweppes	£1 5% Preference	11s 1½d	9·3
Hawker Siddeley	£1 5½% Preference	12s 1½d	9·3
Ranks Hovis	£1 6% Preference	13s 4½d	9·3
British Shoe	£1 6½% Preference	14s 1½d	9·2
Wilmot-Breedon	£1 7% Preference	14s 1½d	10·3

From this he concluded that the company would have to offer
a preference dividend of the order of 10% to market such an issue.

3. A rights issue. This has been traditionally the first choice of the company in the past, although, as the balance sheet shows, it has made substantial use of the other alternatives.

The company's financial advisers estimate that it would be feasible to market the company's shares at about 32s 6d. The present market price of the shares was 37s 6d and the proposed dividend would be 1s 9d per share. Mr Maltby was aware that the indices published showed that the P/E ratio for companies in the capital goods sector was nearly 15.

The rate of Corporation Tax had been increased in the previous budget to the present rate of 45%, and, in view of the forthcoming general election, it was not felt that this would be increased in the short term. There was some uncertainty, however, as far as the long term was concerned. The tax system was under considerable fire, from economists and from the public, as well as from businessmen; and, particularly in view of the prospect of Britain's entry into the Common Market, it was possible that the rate structure of the UK tax system could be changed.

In the past, the company had tended to look at new investment projects in the light of the cost of the new funds that would need to be raised for those projects, and as long as they covered that cost they would be approved. Maltby recently began to doubt this practice, since it tended to ignore the cost of funds generated within the company, and from studies that he has been making of management practice he has come to the conclusion that it is the average cost of capital that should be covered by new investment.

Bob Curtis, the managing director of Pearsons, is not at all happy with this line of thought. He is concerned with pushing forward the projects which he thinks will provide for the future of the company, and as long as these will more than cover the cost of those funds which have to be raised from outside the company he feels that they should be proceeded with. Moreover, he feels that in view of the relative low cost of borrowing, the proportion of the funds to be financed in this way should be pushed up to 30% of the capital employed.

Exhibit 27.1 Pearson Group Limited

Balance Sheets as at 30 June

		1968 £ 000s		1969 £ 000s
Issued Share Capital				
Ordinary Shares of 5s each		2220		2220
Capital Reserves		1558		3708
Retained Profits		2850		3472
		6628		9400
£1 7% Preference Shares		3750		3750
Unsecured Loan 1978–82 8%		4000		4000
		14 378		17 150
Minority Interests		312		340
Future Tax		1040		1188
		£15 730		£18 678
Fixed Assets				
Building and Freehold Land		2762		3120
Plant and Machinery (Net)		9364		10 250
		12 126		13 370
Goodwill		750		750
Current Assets				
Stocks and WIP	2842		4106	
Debtors	4987		6624	
Marketable Securities	642		605	
Cash in Hand	821		791	
	9292		12 126	
Less *Current Liabilities*				
Bank Overdraft	2827		3570	
Creditors	2271		2562	
Tax Due	940		1036	
Final Dividend	400		400	
	6438		7568	
Net Current Assets		2854		4558
Total Funds Employed		£15 730		£18 678

Case Studies in Financial Management

Exhibit 27.2 Pearson Group Limited

Profit and Loss Accounts for the Years to 30 June

		1968		1969
Sales		22 170		29 342
Operating Expenses (Including				
Depreciation 1968 £2331, 1969 £2526)		19 254		26 237
Operating Profit		2916		3105
Interest on Loan		320		320
Net Profit		2596		2785
Tax at 45% (42½% 1968)		1040		1188
Profit after Tax		1556		1597
Minority Interests		24		26
Profits Available to Shareholders		1532		1571
Preference Dividend		262		262
Ordinary Dividends:				
Interim 13%	289		289	
Final 18%	400		400	
		689		689
Increase in Retained Profit		581		620

28

P. P. Payne & Sons Limited*

P. P. Payne & Sons Limited was formed in 1931 when it was incorporated as a private company. Its products include strapping, tapes, and labelling products. The full history of the company is set out in Exhibit 28.1 which shows the data appearing on the Extel cards towards the end of June 1969.

On the 24 July 1969, it was disclosed to the Press that terms had been agreed between Norcros Limited and P. P. Payne for the merger of the two companies by means of an offer from Norcros for the entire issued preference and ordinary capital of P. P. Payne. The full details of this offer were issued on the 13 August 1969, and the offer documents are reproduced in Exhibit 28.2.

Norcros was formed in 1956 to carry on the business of an industrial investment company, and by the date of the offer had built up a group whose activities included prestressed concrete products, kitchen units, pharmaceutical products, coated papers and labels, air-conditioning and refrigeration equipment, and bulk-liquid carriers. Full details of the company are set out in the Extel cards reproduced in Exhibit 28.3.

One financial commentator's view of the bidding Company was given in the *Investors Chronicle* of 15 August 1969 in the following terms:

Norcros Keeping Its End Up

Despite inauspicious trading conditions, Norcros has succeeded

---

*The material appearing in this case is reproduced by kind permission of Norcros Limited, P. P. Payne & Sons Limited, and Hill Samuel & Company Limited.

The Extel Cards are reproduced by kind permission of Extel Statistical Services Limited (The Exchange Telegraph Group).

Comment from the *Investors Chronicle* appears by permission.

The author thanks these organizations for their cooperation in making this case available.

in achieving interim pretax profits of £1·09 million against £998 000 in the half year to 1 January 1968. With the elimination of the Neil and Spencer subsidiary and other unsatisfactory interests, and the acquisition of M and S Shifrin, the results of the two periods are not strictly comparable. But after allowing for adjustments, sales show a 3·7% rise to £12·37 million, which is good going in view of the sharp downturn in UK furniture sales and the lengthy construction industry strike in Canada.

Assuming maintained profits from the established subsidiaries, the acquisition of Shifrin was expected to life profits by £163 000 to around £2·5 million over a full year. Norcros is on its way to this figure and could be further helped by the acquisition of an Australian printing group and of P. P. Payne. This latter company ties in closely with the existing Norprint interests and should provide substantial rationalization benefits.

Rising efficiency should help sustain Norcros until trading conditions begin to improve, as should the increasing proportion of exports and overseas sales. The group began the year with good liquid resources due to recent disposals. Last year's 20·7% dividend (to be held) was well covered by earnings of 32·4%.

At 17s, the 5s shares stand on an historic yield and P/E ratio of 6% and 10·5% respectively. On a medium-term view growth prospects are good and the shares seem undervalued.

Exhibit 28.1 P. P. Payne & Sons Limited

Extel Cards—P. P. Payne & Sons Limited
ANNUAL CARD

PLEASE WITHDRAW PREVIOUS CARD.   COPYRIGHT.

P. P. Payne & Sons Limited
Reg. (Private) 1931. Made Public June 1951.
PRINTED TAPE & GARMENT LABEL MANUFACTURERS, ETC.
Reg. Office: Hadyn Road, Nottingham, NG5 1DL. Tel.: 0602–62221.

Products include:— INDUSTRIAL AND RETAIL PACKAGING DIVISION: 'Tufstrap' Strapping (Non-Adhesive); 'Polystrap' Polypropylene Strapping, Tensioning Tools and Equipment; 'Superseal' Self-Adhesive Strapping Tape; 'Rippatape' Tear Tapes; 'Rippatape' Bag Sealing Tapes, Applicators and Equipment, Weftless Tapes in Cotton and Rayon; LABELLING PRODUCTS DIVISION: Printed Fabric Labels; 'Elegant' Fabric Labels; Printed Self-Adhesive 'Jiffytabs' Labels. REGAL STATIONERY DIVISION: Decorative Tyings, Ribbons, Tags, Seals, Ready-Made Bows and Roses, Industrial and Decorative Ribbons.
SUB. CO.: Tie Tie (Great Britain) Ltd. (Decorative Packaging Distributors).

DIRECTORS: J. E. Payne (Chairman and Managing); O. C. I. Spicer, F.C.W.A. (Deputy-Chairman); L. R. Crawley; C. Radford.

SECRETARY: D. W. Seston, A.C.W.A.

AUTHORISED	CAPITAL	ISSUED & PAID

£150 000 in 8½% (8% to March 31 1966) Cum. Pref. shares of £1 £150 000
£350 000 in Ordinary shares of 5s £250 000

At Dec. 31 1968, Directors' interests (including family interests) in Ord. capital amounted to 55 799 shares.

In June 1951, 50 000 Prefs. and 85 000 Ord. placed at 26s 6d and 13s 3d per share respectively. In Feb. 1954, Capitalisation issue 112 000 Ord. (1 for 5). In May 1961, 268 800 Ord. issued at 14s per share (2 for 5) (xr May 23). In Sept. 1965, 59 200 Ord. shares were issued at 12s 3d per share against options granted to Industrial and Commercial Finance Corpn. Ltd.

VOTING: One vote per £1 Capital but Pref. only in certain circumstances.

DIVIDENDS: Pref. due March 31 and Sept. 30. Pref. entitled to priority for capital with arrears of dividend and premium of 7s 6d per share.

ORD. DIVIDEND PAYMENT DETAILS (Also see below).

Year	%	Announced	Paid	Holders Regd.	Ex Date
1965	Int 5	Oct. 1 1965	Oct. 29	Oct. 2	Oct. 11
	Fin 17	Mar. 8 1966	Mar. 31	Mar. 10	Mar. 14
1966	Int 10	Feb. 21 1966	Apr. 4	Mar. 10	Mar. 14
	Fin 12	Mar. 10 1967	Apr. 5	Mar. 17	Mar. 13
1967	Int 5	Sept. 30 1967	Oct. 31	Oct. 2	Oct. 16
	Fin 10		Apr. 3	Mar. 15	Mar. 25
1968	Int 5	Aug. 15 1968	Oct. 31	Sept. 30	Sept. 16
	Fin 17		Apr. 1	Mar. 7	Feb. 24

DEBENTURE STOCK: 8¼% First Mort. Outstanding Dec. 31 1968, £356 000. All held by Industrial and Commercial Finance Corpn. Ltd. Repayable by annual instalments of £10 000 or whole or part any time after Dec. 31 1972.

ORD. DIVIDENDS OF EARLIER YEARS (%, less tax): 1952, 15; 1953–56, 20; 1957, 22½.

Year ended 30 Sept.	Sales	‡Trading profit &c.	Depn.	Dirs.' emlts.	Bank interest	§Other expenses	Profits tax	Income tax	Corpn. tax
	£ 000s	£	£	£	£	£	£	£	£
¶ 1958 31 Dec.	q	191 556	59 016	40 755	3156	6085	13 750	37 225	—
¶ e1959	q	316 636	63 917	52 455	4538	7694	18 350	60 000	—
¶ 1960	q	236 367	43 841	43 932	q	12 104	14 200	47 500	—
¶ 1961	q	180 153	52 906	37 664	q	18 853	9200	20 800	—
¶ 1962	q	182 850	49 406	37 788	q	21 701	8800	24 700	—
1963	q	216 522	49 531	34 046	q	19 913	17 000	42 700	—
1964	q	253 210	46 448	38 756	—	14 150	22 500	61 000	—
1965	q	289 774	51 975	42 851	—	13 400	—	—	d64 895
1966	q	244 308	44 744	39 991	—	16 343	—	—	d41 000
1967	q	220 142	49 401	35 465	8085	31 665	—	—	g18 000
1968	r2668	361 780	53 580	41 265	14 959	32 247	—	—	s86 500

Year ended 30 Sept.	Net profit after tax	Profit after pref. div.	% On ordinary less tax		Retd. by sub. cos.	Appropriations Gen. res.	Other	No. of employees
	£	£	*Earned	Paid	£	£	£	
¶ 1958 31 Dec.	31 569	24 669	25·5	Int 5 Fin 15	M4144	h 6000	Mi 4611	q
¶ e1959	110 182	101 220	b98·4	Int 5 Sec. Int 5 Fin 15	—	h 6000	Mi 1600	q

¶ 1960	**74 790**	67 440	65·5	Int 5 Fin 15	908	a10 000	h 6000	q
							c12 310	
¶ 1961	**40 730**	33 380	23·2	Int 5 Fin 15	1237	a15 000	h 6000	q
¶ 1962	**40 455**	33 105	23·0	Int 5 Fin 7½	233	h10 000	j17 575	q
1963	**53 332**	45 982	31·9	Int 5 Fin 12½		15 000	j 7705	q
						h10 000	Mn 4856	q
1964	**70 356**	63 006	43·7	Int 5 Fin 15		15 000	h10 000	q
1964			p35·3					
1965	**116 653**	109 528	44·5	Int 5 Fin 17		35 000	h10 000	q ·
							Mi 8921	
1966	**102 230**	89 668	35·9	Int u 10 Fin 12		—	Mk10 939	q
1967	**77 526**	64 776	25·9	Int 5 Fin 10		—	—	699
1968	**133 229**	120 479	48·2	Int 5 Fin 17		30 000	Mi 6240	t747
						a25 000		

ISSUED ORDINARY was £168 000 from 1958 to 1960, £235 200 from 1961 to 1965 and £250 000 from 1966 to 1968.

Note: Charge for taxation is after crediting relief due to Investment Allowances of £5183 in 1964, £8362 in 1965, £12 953 in 1966 and £9756 in 1967.

*After charging profits tax to the extent provided in Accounts. ‡After deducting overseas taxation. §Deb. and other Interest, Audit Fees, etc. ¶ Consolidated profit and loss account. (a) New product development reserve. (b) Equivalent to 78·7% p.a. (c) Cost of launching new products during year. (d) At 40%. (e) 15 months. (g) At 42%. (h) Deb. redemption reserve. (i) Taxation provision no longer required. (j) Sub. Cos. and polythene closure reserve after tax. (k) Income tax deducted from dividends and retained. (n) Provisions for Sub. Cos. (p) Estimated Earnings after allowing for Corporation Tax at 40%. (q) Not disclosed. (r) Including exports of £441 075. (s) At 42½%. (t) Average number; remuneration, £742 475. (u) On £235 200 capital and includes 5% paid in order to maximise tax benefits arising from changeover to Corporation Tax. M—Minus.

PRIORITY PERCENTAGES:

	Deb. Stock (Net)	8% Cum. Pref.	Ordinary	Retd. Profit	Total Earnings
†1966	£9416	£12 562	£53 520	£36 148	£111 646
1967	17 834	12 750	37 500	27 276	95 360
1968	⎰ 18 168	12 750	55 000	65 479	151 397
	%	%	%	%	—
	⎱ 0–12	12–20½	20½–56¾	56¾–100	—

†Dividends shown gross though partly net in accounts.

CONSOLIDATED HALF YEARLY FIGURES. To June 30.

	Trading Profit	Depreciation	Finance Charges	Profit before Tax
1965	£100 638	£20 205	£4342	£76 091
1966	£110 806	£30 647	£5062	£75 097
1967	£69 543	£21 577	£15 868	£32 098
1968	£144 456	£26 328	£22 701	£95 427

LONDON PRICES OF 5s ORDINARY SHARES.

Cal. year	1960	1961	1962	1963	1964	1965	1966	1967	1968	*1969
Highest	21s 0d	19s 0d	14s 3d	12s 9d	15s 3d	15s 6d	19s 0d	17s 3d	23s 3d	22s 9d
Lowest	13s 0d	13s 6d	9s 0d	8s 7d	11s 1d	11s 7d	14s 1d	12s 6d	12s 6d	20s 7d

*To 17 Feb.

GROSS YIELD INDICATOR 22% Dividend. 48·2% Earnings. £250 000 Capital.

PRICE		19s 0d	20s 0d	21s 0d	22s 0d	23s 0d	24s 0d	25s 0d	26s 0d	27s 0d
DIVIDEND YIELD	%	5·79	5·50	5·24	5·00	4·78	4·58	4·40	4·23	4·07
EARNINGS YIELD	%	12·68	12·05	11·48	10·95	10·48	10·04	9·64	9·27	8·93
PRICE/EARNINGS RATIO		7·88	8·30	8·71	9·13	9·54	9·96	10·37	10·79	11·20

BALANCE SHEETS. 31 DECEMBER.

	1967	1968		1967	1968
	£	£		£	£
CAPITAL	400 000	400 000	CURRENT ASSETS		
CAPITAL RESERVES			Stock	364 549	402 103
Share Prem. A/c.	146 045	146 045	Debtors, etc.	486 331	428 849
Asset Revaluation			Cash	220	70 048
and General	119 199	119 199			
REVENUE RESERVES				851 100	901 000
General	140 000	170 000	CURRENT LIABS.	496 717	*492 551
Development Res.	25 000	50 000			
Appropriation A/c.	295 658	312 377	NET CURT. ASSETS	354 383	408 449
MORTGAGE DEB.	383 000	356 000	FIXED ASSETS	1 154 519	†1 145 172
	£1 508 902	£1 553 621		£1 508 902	£1 553 621

*Creditors £349 150 (1967, £256 125); H.P. Creditors Nil (£26 710); Taxation £97 714 (£55 882); Overdraft Nil (£129 813); Pref. Dividend £3187 (£3187); Final Ord. Dividend £42 500 (£25 000). †Gross Value: Freehold Properties £846 442 (after deducting £14 131 investment grant); Leasehold Properties £51 054 (after deducting £5975 investment grant and £6120 depreciation); Plant and Machinery £159 087 (after deducting £27 174 investment grant and £444 617 depreciation; Fixtures and Fittings £31 200 (after deducting £1309 investment grant and £99 503 depreciation); Vehicles £57 389 (after £34 284 depreciation).

Note (1968): Gross value of Assets is at cost, except Plant and Machinery and Freehold Properties, which are at valuation to Sept. 30 1941 and Dec. 31 1961 respectively, with subsequent additions at cost.

NET ASSET VALUE (BOOK VALUE), excluding intangibles, at B/s. date per 5s Ord. share: 1968, 19s 10d.

Aug. 15 1968.

INTERIM DIVIDEND of 5%, less tax, on Ord. shares on account of year 1968, payable Oct. 31 to holders registered Sept. 30 (5 p.m.). Books closed Oct. 1–4. (xd Sept. 16).

Nov. 27 1968.

SALE OF PART OF 'REGAL' DIVISION. Agreement has been reached with Valentine & Sons Ltd.—a wholly owned Sub. Co. of John Waddington Ltd.—on terms for sale of Co.'s interest in Gift Wrap and Dressings market, represented by part of 'Regal' Division. Board have been seriously concerned with intensified competition from Greetings Card Manufacturers who lately have integrated Greetings Cards and Gift-Wrappings marketing with very large resources behind them. Co. have been publishers only of Wrappings, Papers, Tags, Seals and Social Stationery lines, thus being at a disadvantage

177

in competing with actual printers and reducing margins in consequence. With
need to increase profitability of this range Board had to consider whether cost
of installing a large plant for printing could be warranted in order to cater for
manufacture of above products and also add Greetings Cards to range to
effectively combat above mentioned competition. In addition to heavy capital
cost of plant 'very large' additional factory accommodation would be required
to house the printing plant, raw materials, manufactured goods and packed
goods for later delivery because of their seasonal nature and large bulk. An
evaluation of overall financial resources at Co.'s disposal had to be made with
need to cater also for expansion of their ranges of packaging and Labelling
Products. These are not only more profitable, but have 'very considerable'
growth potential. In view of these circumstances and after discussion with
their Deb. Holders and Advisers Board decided to streamline Co.'s activities
by disposing of 'Gift Wrap and Dressings' element of 'Regal' range but retaining Gift Ribbon plant. A satisfactory offer was received from John Waddington
Ltd. for integration with their Valentine's Greetings Card Sub. Co. for sum
of £140 000 for 'Goodwill', Plant and Machinery £2000, all stocks at book
value—estimated to be approx. £150 000 on take-over date and a long-term
Agreement was negotiated at same time to purchase their Gift Ribbon requirements exclusively from Co. at a fair market price, enabling Co. to retain current
volume of Gift Ribbon business as a result.

Effective date of transaction will be Jan. 6 1969 and all consideration money
will be paid in cash by completion date. Net profit contribution from section
of 'Regal' Division being transferred amounted to approx. 20% of Co. total
of £95 526, before taxation, for last financial year to Dec. 31 1967. Forecasts
already made concerning profit and dividend expectations of 22% for 1968
are not affected by this transaction.

Redeployment of proceeds from transaction, together with additional
factory space made available, will be effectively utilised in expansion of established more profitable Packaging and Labelling products, addition of further
new complementary lines and to reduce their indebtedness to their bankers
which was mainly required to finance seasonal aspect of 'Regal' trading. These
factors will be very beneficial to Co.'s growth prospects for 1969/1970 onwards. It is opinion of Board that this 'streamlining' will be of 'long term'
benefit to future profitability of Co. and enable still more intense concentra-
tion in their specialised Packaging and Labelling activities and expansion of
their leadership in these respective fields.
March 11 1969.
REPORT for year ended Dec. 31 1968. For figures, see tables. Final dividend
of 17%, less tax, on Ord., making 22% for year, payable Apr. 1. Books closed
Mar. 8 to 12 (xd Feb. 24). Carry forward £312 377 (£295 658).
FINANCE ACT, 1965. Close Co. provisions of Act do not apply to this
Company in opinion of Directors.

Meeting, George Hotel, George Street, Nottingham, Apr. 1 at 2.30 p.m.

P. P. Payne & Sons Limited

CHAIRMAN'S STATEMENT. Trading conditions during year have been
in sharp contrast to those of preceding year, and can—as far as their Labelling,

Packaging and Decorative Ribbon Product ranges are concerned—only be described as 'excellent' with a 'sharp' increase in turnover in all sections, thus enabling Company to reap benefit from new plant installed during past year. Utilisation to maximum of this capacity, together with implementation of 'productivity' incentive schemes has produced a considerable improvement in 'profitability' in these sections of their activities in spite of higher labour costs and other increases with which they have had to contend from nationalised services.

PROSPECTS. Board, given any stable trading conditions during current year, anticipate with utmost confidence, a continuation of expansion achieved during 1968, and which is expected to yield further improved results on those for year under review. All of the products they are now selling are wholly manufactured by Co. and Order and Invoice Sales for these lines are in advance of comparative period last year.

LATER INFORMATION WILL BE PUBLISHED ON NEWS CARD.

Extel Statistical Services Limited, Extel House, East Harding Street, London EC4. The Exchange Telegraph Daily Statistics Service. Telephone: Manager—SHOreditch 2041. Extra Cards only: (91 Moorgate, London EC2.) Telephone: NATional 0754. This information, while not guaranteed, is believed to be correct.

NEWS CARD

P. P. Payne & Sons Limited

NEWS CARD   UP-DATED TO 4–9–69.

PA-PD 70   Please withdraw previous News Card

GROSS YIELD INDICATOR based on 22% Dividend. 48·2% (2·41s per share) Earnings. £250 000 Capital.

PRICE	27s 6d	30s 0d	32s 6d	35s 0d	37s 6d	40s 0d	42s 6d
DIVIDEND YIELD %	4·00	3·28	3·38	3·14	2·93	2·75	2·59
EARNINGS YIELD %	8·76	8·03	7·42	6·89	6·43	6·03	5·67
P/E RATIO	11·41	12·45	13·49	14·52	15·56	16·60	17·63

SHARE PRICES. 5s ORD. (LONDON): 1969, Highest 34s, Lowest 20s 7d. To Aug. 18.

ORD. DIVIDEND PAYMENT DETAILS. Year end Dec. 31. Last accounts published March 11 1969

	%	Per Share	Announced	Paid	Holders	Ex Date
1966	Int 10	6d	Feb. 21 1966	Apr. 4	Mar. 10	Mar. 14
1966	Fin 12	7s 2d	Mar. 10 1967	Apr. 5	Mar. 17	Mar. 13
1967	Int 5	3d	Sept. 30 1967	Oct. 31	Oct. 2	Oct. 16
1967	Fin 10	6d	Mar. 8 1968	Apr. 3	Mar. 15	Mar. 25
1968	Int 5	3d	Aug. 15 1968	Oct. 31	Sept. 30	Sept. 16
1968	Fin 17	10s 2d	Mar. 11 1969	Apr. 1	Mar. 14	Mar. 24
1969	Int 10	6d	14–8–69	16–9–69	2–9–69	18–8–69

CONSOLIDATED HALF YEARLY FIGURES. To June 30.

	Trading Profit	Deprecia-tion	Finance Charges	Profit before Tax
1966	£110 806	£30 647	£5062	£75 097
1967	£69 543	£21 577	£15 868	£32 098
1968	£144 456	£26 328	£22 701	£95 427
1969	£181 282	£27 379	£13 041	£140 862

MEETING. Chairman said that sale of Regal 'Gift-Wrap' section left a gap in Co's annual turnover, which had been more than adequately recovered from most satisfactory increased sales of labelling, packaging and decorative ribbon products. Continued efforts made in this direction, subject always of course to any further economic restrictions which might be imposed in coming Budget, were expected, under normal trading conditions for remainder of this year, to show an improvement on present figures. Exports so far this year were up by 40%.

Exhibit 28.2 Offers by Hill Samuel & Co. Limited on behalf of Norcros Limited

P. P. Payne & Sons Limited

Directors:
J. E. Payne (Chairman and Managing)
O. C. I. Spicer, F.C.W.A. (Deputy Chairman)
L. R. Crawley
C. Radford

Haydn Road,
Nottingham, NG5 1DL

13th August 1969

To the Ordinary and Preference shareholders

Dear Sir or Madam,
OFFERS BY NORCROS LIMITED

It was announced in the Press on 24th July that the Directors of your Company and the Directors of Norcros Limited ('Norcros') had reached agreement for the two companies to be merged by means of Offers by Norcros to acquire the whole of the issued Preference and Ordinary share capital of your Company. Details of these Offers are set out in the formal Offer Document accompanying this letter.

If the merger becomes effective it is intended that your Company will continue to operate under its existing management as an important part of the printing division of Norcros, the major operating company of which is Norprint Limited. I, together with the Deputy Chairman, Mr O. C. I. Spicer, will join the Board of Norprint Limited and an assurance has been received to the effect that the interests of all management and staff, including pension rights, will be fully safeguarded.

The profits before tax of your Company for the first six months of the current year as shown by the interim unaudited accounts at 5th July 1969 amounted to £140,862 as compared with £95,427 for the corresponding period of the previous year. Although forecasting profits in the present economic climate is not easy, your Directors expect that in the absence of unforeseen circumstances, profits before tax for the year to 31st December 1969 are likely to be of the order of £250,000. In making this forecast, your Directors have assumed that the level of turnover during the second six months of the current year will be maintained at the level foreshadowed by the Company's budgets and that there will, during the same period, be no significant increases in the level of direct costs and general overheads.

Preference Share Offer

Preference shareholders are offered £1 in cash for each $8\frac{1}{2}\%$ Cumulative Preference share of £1 which represents an increase in value of more than 14% compared with the middle market quotation on the day before the Offers were announced.

Ordinary Share Offer

Your attention is drawn to page 5 from which you will see that Ordinary shareholders are being offered 35s per share in cash or, alternatively, partly cash and partly shares in Norcros having a value approximately equivalent to 31s 9d per share. Your Directors believe that if your Company were to continue as an independent entity it would be some years before the Ordinary shares commanded a price on The Stock Exchange, London, approaching the 35s per share now offered in cash by Norcros.

Your Directors who have been advised by Kleinwort, Benson Limited, having carefully considered these Offers, believe them to be fair and reasonable and unanimously recommend all shareholders to accept. They do not feel able, however, to advise Ordinary shareholders as to which of the two alternatives they should accept since much may depend upon an individual's circumstances in relation to capital gains tax. Ordinary shareholders should, therefore, consult their professional advisers if they are in doubt as to which course of action they should adopt. However, your Directors intend to accept the ALL cash offer in respect of their own holdings totalling 11,703 Ordinary shares and 300 Preference shares.

Yours faithfully,
J. E. PAYNE,
Chairman

100 Wood Street,
London, E.C.2
13th August 1969

Hill Samuel & Co. Limited

To the Ordinary and Preference shareholders of
P. P. PAYNE & SONS LIMITED

Dear Sir or Madam,

OFFERS BY NORCROS LIMITED

It was announced in the press on 24th July 1969 that the Boards of Norcros Limited ('Norcros') and P. P. Payne & Sons Limited ('Payne') had agreed the terms of a merger under which Payne would become a member of the Norcros Group. The merger is to be effected by means of Offers on behalf of Norcros, the terms of which are set out below, to acquire the whole of the issued share capital of Payne.

There is set out on page 2 a letter from Mr J. E. Payne, the Chairman of Payne, which forms part of this Offer document. As stated therein the Directors of Payne are unanimously of the opinion that the terms of the Offers are fair and reasonable and recommend all shareholders to accept.

Colebrook Nominees Limited, a wholly owned subsidiary of Hill Samuel & Co. Limited, the holder of approximately 24·1% of the Ordinary shares of Payne, intends to accept the Norcros Offer in respect of those shares.

1. THE OFFERS

At the request of Norcros and on its behalf we hereby offer to acquire the whole of the issued Ordinary and Preference share capital of Payne, comprising 1,000,000 Ordinary shares of 5s each and 150,000 8½% Cumulative Preference shares of £1 each, on the terms and conditions set out below:—

Terms of the Offers

Shares in Payne	*Consideration Offered*
For EACH Ordinary share of 5s	**35s 0d in cash**
For EACH 8½%	
Cumulative Preference share of £1	**20s 0d in cash**

Share Alternative

An accepting Ordinary shareholder of Payne may elect to receive, instead of wholly cash:—

Shares in Payne	*Consideration Offered*
For every TEN Ordinary shares of 5s each	**NINE Ordinary shares of 5s each of Norcros**
	and
	160s 0d in cash

and so in proportion for any other number of Ordinary shares of Payne. The Share Alternative may be chosen in respect of all or any of the Ordinary shares of Payne comprised in any acceptance. **The Share Alternative will only be available until 10 a.m. on 3rd September 1969 and will not be extended beyond that date.**

Fractions.—In cases where Ordinary shareholders of Payne would become entitled to a fraction of an Ordinary share of Norcros, such fractions will be aggregated and sold and the net proceeds of sale distributed *pro rata* to the persons entitled thereto.

Quotation.—Application will be made to the Council of The Stock Exchange, London, for permission to deal in and for quotation for the new Ordinary shares of Norcros to be issued under the Share Alternative.

Dividends.—The Ordinary and Preference shares of Payne are to be acquired free from all liens, charges and encumbrances, and with the right to all dividends and other rights now or hereafter attaching thereto, except that:

(i) The holders of Ordinary shares on the register on 2nd September 1969 will be entitled to retain an interim dividend of 10% which will be paid on 16th September 1969 in respect of the year ending 31st December 1969.

(ii) The holders of Preference shares on the register on 2nd September 1969 will be entitled to retain the dividend of 4¼% which will be paid on 16th September 1969 in respect of the six months ending on 30th September 1969.

New Ordinary shares of Norcros issued under the Share Alternative will be credited as fully paid and will rank *pari passu* in all respects with the Ordinary shares of Norcros at present in issue except that they will not be entitled to the interim dividend of 8·33% announced today for payment on 29th November 1969.

Conditions of the Offers

The Offers, which are to be treated as separate offers for each class of share capital of Payne, are subject to the following conditions:—

(a) In the case of each class of share capital:—
acceptance by 10 a.m. on 3rd September 1969, or such later date being not later than 12th October 1969 (the latest date on which the Offers may be declared unconditional) as Norcros may decide, in respect of not less than 90% of the issued shares of the class, or such less percentage subject to paragraph 4(A) of Appendix III as Norcros may decide.

(b) In the case of the Ordinary share capital:—
permission to deal in and quotation for the Ordinary shares of Norcros to be issued pursuant to the Share Alternative being granted by the Council of The Stock Exchange, London (subject to allotment), within 14 days of the Offer becoming otherwise unconditional.

(c) In the case of the Preference share capital:—
the Offer for the Ordinary shares becoming unconditional.

Further terms and information in connection with the Offers are set out in Appendix III.

2. BUSINESS OF THE TWO COMPANIES

Norcros

Norcros, which was incorporated in 1956, is the controlling company of an Industrial Group organised in operating divisions having the following principal subsidiaries:—

Construction and Engineering Division

Dow-Mac Concrete Limited—A leading specialist designer and manufacturer of pre-cast pre-stressed reinforced concrete products for the building and construction industries including railway sleepers, beams for motorway bridges and fly-overs.

Temperature Limited—Manufacturers of a wide range of air-conditioning and refrigeration equipment including multi-room applications and environmental control engineering for the Armed Forces.

Consumer Products Division

Hygena Limited—A brand leader and the largest manufacturer of fitted

183

kitchen storage units in the United Kingdom.

M. & S. Shifrin Limited—Manufacturers of dining room and bedroom furniture.

S. Maw, Son & Sons Limited—Maws is a household name in baby and nursery products. A range of toiletry products under the brand name 'Softcare' has recently been launched.

Lantigen (England) Limited—Manufacturers of bacterial vaccines for oral application, the best known being 'Lantigen B'.

Printing Division

Norprint Limited—Manufacturers of tickets, labels and tags using the latest printing techniques for application on to almost every type of paper, film and foil. A range of machines, applicators and dispensers are supplied which print and apply labels for use in stores, supermarkets and industry. Other important products of the Division are specialised coated papers and films for the printing industry for use in the production of photogravure cylinders and screens for silk screen printing.

Norcros has a number of overseas interests of which the largest is its subsidiary Bulk Carriers Limited of Toronto, Canada. It is one of the largest road transport companies in Canada and is concerned with the transport of liquid and dry products in bulk, mainly in eastern Canada and the neighbouring States of the USA.

Financial information concerning Norcros is set out in Appendix I.

Payne

Payne, which became a public quoted company in 1951, carries on a business originally established in 1870. At its modern factories in Nottingham, Payne manufactures printed labels on a variety of acetate and cotton materials which are used extensively in the textile and clothing industries including a new range of highly successful screen printed cloth labels under the trade name 'Elegant'. The Company also manufactures printed tags on board and paper, strapping materials in rayon and polypropylene, decorative ribbons and other complementary products.

Financial information concerning Payne is set out in Appendix II.

The Merger

Payne's business forms a logical extension of the printing division of Norcros. The two organisations' product ranges are complementary and it is expected that benefits from the integration of their activities in marketing, production and distribution will result in increased overall profitability.

It is intended that following the merger Payne will continue to operate under its present management as part of the printing division of Norcros and that the interests of all management and staff, including pension rights, will be fully safeguarded.

3. PROFITS AND DIVIDENDS

Norcros

The Norcros Interim Report for the 26 weeks ended 1st June 1969 shows that:

Group sales were £12,368,000 compared with £11,923,000 over the corresponding period for 1968 after adjusting for companies since sold and the acquisition of M. & S. Shifrin Limited. The increase represents an improvement of 3·7%.

Unaudited group profits before taxation and minority interests increased by 8·8% over the half-year to £1,086,000 compared with £998,000 for the corresponding period last year for the Group as then constituted.

Earnings for Ordinary shareholders for the 26 weeks ended 1st June 1969 increased to £524,000, representing 8·2d per share after providing for Corporation Tax at 45%. Last year over the corresponding period the earnings were £512,000 representing 8·0d per share after providing tax at the previous rate of $42\frac{1}{2}\%$.

The Directors of Norcros envisage that, in the absence of unforeseen circumstances Ordinary dividends for the year ending 1st December 1969 will amount to not less than 20·7% (1968—20·7%) of which an interim dividend of 8·33% will be paid on 29th November 1969.

The Ordinary shares of Norcros issued under the Share Alternative will not rank for this interim dividend.

Payne

As stated on page 2 of this document, the profits before tax of Payne for the first six months of the current year as shown by the interim unaudited accounts of 5th July 1969 amounted to £140,862, as compared with £95,427 for the corresponding period of the previous year. The Directors expect that profits before tax for the year ending 31st December 1969 are likely to be of the order of £250,000.

4. EFFECT OF ACCEPTANCE
ORDINARY SHARES
Value of the Cash Offer

The Cash Offer values each Ordinary share of Payne at 35s 0d. On the basis of the middle-market quotation as shown in the Daily Official List of The Stock Exchange, London, for the Ordinary shares of Payne on 23rd July 1969 (the day preceding the announcement of the Offer) of 21s 6d, **this represents an increase in value of more than 60%.**

Value of the Share Alternative

Based on the middle-market quotations as shown in the Daily Official List of The Stock Exchange, London, for the Ordinary shares of Payne on 23rd July 1969 and for the Ordinary shares of Norcros on 8th August 1969 (the last practicable date prior to the printing of this document) the effect of acceptance of the Offer on a holder of 10 Ordinary shares of Payne who elects for the Share Alternative would be:—

Before Acceptance		*After Acceptance*	
Market value of 10 Payne Ordinary shares of 5s at 21s 6d	215s 0d	Market value of 9 Norcros Ordinary shares of 5s at 17s 6d	157s 6d
		Cash	160s 0d
	215s 0d		317s 6d

This represents an increase in value of more than 47%.
Further Stock Exchange quotations are shown in Appendix III.

Income of Acceptors of the Cash Offer
On the basis of the Ordinary dividends paid by Payne in respect of the year ended 31st December 1968, and on the assumption that the cash proceeds (ignoring the incidence of capital gains tax, if any) were reinvested at the rate of 7% per annum, the gross income of a holder of 10 Ordinary shares of Payne who accepts the Offer would be increased as follows:—

Before Acceptance		*After Acceptance*	
Dividend on 10 Payne		Interest on 350s 0d	
Ordinary shares at 22%	11s 0d	cash at 7%	24s 6d

This represents an increase in gross income of more than 122%.

Income of Acceptors of the Share Alternative
On the basis of Ordinary dividends of Norcros aggregating 20·7%, and on the assumption that the cash proceeds (ignoring the incidence of capital gains tax, if any) were reinvested at the rate of 7% per annum, the gross income in a full year of a holder of 10 Ordinary shares of Payne who elects for the Share Alternative would be increased as follows:—

Before Acceptance		*After Acceptance*	
Dividend on 10 Payne		Dividend on 9 Norcros	
Ordinary shares at 22%	11s 0d	Ordinary shares at 20·7%	9s 4d
		Interest on 160s in cash	
		at 7%	11s 2d
	11s 0d		20s 6d

This represents an increase in gross income of more than 86%.

PREFERENCE SHARES
The Preference Offer valued each Preference share of Payne at 20s 0d compared with a market value of 17s 6d on 23rd July 1969 (the day preceding the announcement of the Offer).

This represents an increase in value of more than 14%.

5. CAPITAL GAINS TAX
Acceptance of the Offers will constitute a disposal for the purposes of capital gains tax and liability to tax will depend on the circumstances of the individual shareholder. Shareholders of Payne are advised to consult their professional advisers if they are in any doubt as to their individual tax position.

The 'market values' on 6th April 1965 of one Ordinary share and of one Preference share of Payne were 13s 6d and 20s 6d respectively.

6. HOW TO ACCEPT
Cash Offers
If you wish to accept the Offer for the class of shares held by you, the enclosed Form(s) of Acceptance and Transfer (white for Ordinary shares, pink for Preference shares) must be completed and signed in accordance with the instructions thereon and returned, together with the relative share certi-

ficate(s) of Payne, in the enclosed stamped addressed envelope to Hill Samuel & Co. Limited, 6 Greencoat Place, London, S.W.1. **Please send them so as to arrive not later than 10 a.m. on Wednesday, 3rd September 1969.**

Share Alternative

If you wish to elect for the Share Alternative in respect of all or any of your Ordinary shares of Payne the relevant part(s) of the white Form of Acceptance and Transfer must be completed, signed and returned together with your share certificate(s) of Payne in the enclosed stamped addressed envelope to Hill Samuel & Co. Limited, 6 Greencoat Place, London, S.W.1. **Please send them so as to arrive not later than 10 a.m. on Wednesday, 3rd September 1969.**

If your share certificate(s) is/are not readily available the relevant Form of Acceptance and Transfer should nevertheless be completed and returned in the accompanying envelope, and the share certificate(s) forwarded as soon as possible. Norcros reserves the right to treat acceptances as valid even though not accompanied by the relevant share certificate(s).

7. SETTLEMENT

If you are a holder of Ordinary shares of Payne and your Form of Acceptance and Transfer and share certificate(s) are in order, there will be sent to you or your agent by post within 7 days of the Ordinary share Offer becoming unconditional, or the receipt of the documents complete in all respects, whichever is the later, a cheque for the cash consideration for your Ordinary shares together with, in the case of shareholders electing for the Share Alternative, a renounceable letter of allotment for the Ordinary shares of Norcros to which you will have become entitled, and a remittance in respect of fractions (if any).

If you are a holder of Preference shares of Payne and your Form of Acceptance and Transfer and share certificate(s) are in order, there will be sent to you or your agent by post within 7 days of the Offer for the Preference shares becoming unconditional, or the receipt of the documents complete in all respects, which ever is the later, a cheque for the cash consideration for your Preference shares.

No other acknowledgement of your Form(s) of Acceptance and Transfer and share certificate(s) will be given.

If the Offer which you have accepted does not become unconditional your share certificate(s) together with the appropriate Form of Acceptance and Transfer will be returned to you by post within 14 days of such Offer lapsing.

Yours faithfully,
HILL SAMUEL & CO. LIMITED,
L. H. L. COHEN,
Director.

Norcros Limited

Registered Office: Reading Bridge House, Reading, Berkshire.

1. SHARE CAPITAL

The authorised and issued share capital of Norcros assuming full acceptance of the Share Alternative would be:—

Authorised £		£	Issued and fully paid £
4,000,000	6½% Cumulative Preference shares of £1 each		2,198,327
6,000,000	Ordinary shares of 5s each:		
	Already in issue	3,821,675	
	Maximum which can be issued under Share Alternative	225,000	
			4,046,675
£10,000,000			£6,245,002

2. PROFITS AND ORDINARY DIVIDENDS

The following table shows the consolidated profits before taxation of Norcros and its subsidiaries as shown by the audited accounts for, and the rate of Ordinary dividends paid by Norcros in respect of, each of the five financial periods ended 1st December 1968.

	Issued ordinary capital £ 000s	Annual dividend rate %	Profits before taxation £ 000s
1964	3,820	20·0	2,066
1965	3,822	20·0	1,933
1966	3,822	20·0	1,904
1967	3,822	20·0	1,879
1968	3,822	20·7	2,361

3. NET TANGIBLE ASSETS

The consolidated net tangible assets of Norcros and its subsidiaries based on the audited accounts at 1st December 1968, were:—

	£ 000s	£ 000s
Fixed Assets		
Freehold properties		2,814
Leasehold properties		1,045
Plant, machinery and equipment		3,126
		6,985

Investments		
Quoted (market value £359,000)	263	
Unquoted	92	
		355
Current Assets		
Stocks	4,210	
Debtors	7,230	
Cash at bankers and in hand	318	
	11,758	
Less *Current Liabilities*		
Creditors and hire purchase instalments	5,270	
Bank overdrafts	1,257	
Dividends	473	
	7,000	
Net Current Assets		4,758
		12,098
Less:		
Minority interests	244	
Loan capital	2,622	
Tax equalisation	374	
Corporation Tax due January 1970	808	
		4,048
Net Tangible Assets		£8,050

Since 1st December 1968:—

(i) Norcros has acquired M. & S. Shifrin Limited for £2,000,000 which has been satisfied by the issue of £2,000,000 5% Unsecured Loan Stock 1969/71;

(ii) Norcros, through its wholly-owned Australian subsidiary, Sorcron Pty. Limited, has acquired 70% of the share capital of Raymond Holdings Pty. Limited of Sydney, Australia, for a cash consideration of £245,000;

(iii) Norcros has sold Neil and Spencer Limited, a wholly-owned subsidiary, for a cash consideration of £1,560,000, the purchaser repaying loans due to Norcros of £1,440,000;

(iv) Norcros has sold two wholly-owned subsidiaries for an aggregate cash consideration of £32,559, the purchasers repaying loans due to Norcros of £199,556;

(v) Norcros has announced Earnings for Ordinary shareholders of £524,000 (subject to audit) for the 26 weeks ended 1st June 1969 and an interim dividend for the current year which will absorb £318,000.

The changes arising from the above transactions amount to a diminution in net tangible assets estimated at £721,000. Apart from these changes and changes arising from transactions in the ordinary course of business the present financial position is not materially different from that shown above.

P. P. Payne & Sons Limited

Registered Office: Haydn Road, Nottingham

1. SHARE CAPITAL

The authorised and issued share capital of Payne is:—

Authorised £		Issued and fully paid £
150,000	8½% Cumulative Preference shares of £1 each	150,000
350,000	Ordinary shares of 5s each	250,000
£500,000		£400,000

The coupon on the Preference shares was increased from 8% to 8½% with effect from 1st April 1966.

2. PROFITS AND ORDINARY DIVIDENDS

The following table shows the profits before taxation of Payne as shown by the audited accounts for, and the rate of Ordinary dividends paid by Payne in respect of, each of the five years ended 31st December 1968.

	Issued ordinary capital £ 000s	Annual dividend rate %	Profits before taxation £ 000s
1964	235	20	154
1965	235	22	182
1966	250	22	143
1967	250	15	96
1968	250	22	220

3. NET TANGIBLE ASSETS

The net tangible assets of Payne based on the audited accounts at 31st December 1968, were:—

Fixed Assets	£ 000s	£ 000s
Freehold properties		846
Leasehold properties		51
Plant, machinery and equipment		248
		1,145
Current Assets		
Stocks	402	
Debtors less adjustment	429	
Bank balances and cash	70	
	901	

Less *Current Liabilities*
Creditors	349
Current taxation	98
Dividend	46

493

Net Current Assets   408

1,553

Less:
Mortgage Debenture   356

Net Tangible Assets   £1,197

Since 31st December 1968, the net tangible assets of Payne have been increased by the sum of £140,000 (against which must be set certain expenses and Capital Gains Tax yet to be determined) arising on the sale of the 'Gift-Wrap and Dressings' element of the 'Regal' range to John Waddington Limited. Apart from this transaction, transactions in the ordinary course of business and the increase in net assets resulting from retained earnings, the present financial position of Payne is not materially different from that shown above.

APPENDIX III
Additional Information
1. INTERESTS

(i) Neither Norcros nor any of its subsidiaries nor any of its Directors is beneficially interested in the share capital of Payne.

(ii) The Directors of Norcros and their families are interested in the following shares of Norcros:—

	Ordinary 5s shares of Norcros
J. V. Sheffield	2,666
J. J. Boex	1,199
F. J. Briggs	1,215
D. Kirkness	2,500
P. I. Marshall	5,000
The Hon. P. M. Samuel	400
E. C. R. Sheffield	12,771
W. G. S. Tozer	2,800

(iii) Neither Payne nor its subsidiary nor any of its Directors is beneficially interested in the share capital of Norcros with the exception of Mr O. C. I.

Note:—At 1st December 1968, Mr J. V. Sheffield and Mr E. C. R. Sheffield held through Independent Investment Trust Limited, a company controlled by their families, 993,800 Ordinary shares in Norcros. Independent Investment Trust Limited has since been acquired by Atlantic Assets Trust Limited of which Mr J. V. Sheffield is a Director.

Spicer who purchased 2500 Ordinary shares of Norcros at an average price of 15s 1d per share on 30th July 1969.

(iv) The Directors of Payne and their families are interested in the following shares of Payne:—

	Ordinary shares	Preference shares
J. E. Payne	7,000	—
O. C. I. Spicer	2,518	250
L. R. Crawley	1,545	100
C. Radford	640	—

No shares in Payne were purchased by the Directors during the six months immediately prior to the date of this Offer Letter with the exception of 165 Ordinary shares purchased by Mr J. E. Payne at a price of 24s per share on 2nd May 1969.

(v) Since 24th July 1969, certain shareholders of Payne, some of whom are associates of Directors of Payne, have sold Ordinary shares at a price of 35s per share and Preference shares at a price of 20s per share to Colebrook Nominees Limited ('Colebrook') amounting in aggregate to 241,012 Ordinary shares and 1,100 Preference shares. Colebrook, which has agreed to account to the vendors for the interim Ordinary dividend of Payne payable on 16th September 1969, intends to accept the Cash Offer for the Ordinary shares.

Hill Samuel & Co. Limited purchased 7,500 Ordinary shares of Payne as follows:—

Date	Number	Average Price
29th July 1969	2,500	34s 0d
31st July 1969	5,000	34s 0d

Hill Samuel & Co. Limited intends to accept the Cash Offer for the above shares.

2. SERVICE CONTRACTS

(i) There are no agreements or arrangements arising from or in connection with the Offers under which the emoluments of any of the Directors of Norcros will be varied. The emoluments of the Directors of Norcros for the year ended 1st December 1968, amounted to £86,962, of which £14,131 was paid to certain Directors holding executive office, by way of profit sharing incentive determined by reference to the improvement in earnings for Ordinary shareholders, in exercise of the Board's power to make such payments. The Board may resolve to make similar payments in respect of the year ending 30th November 1969 and subsequent years.

(ii) No Director of Norcros has a service contract which is not determinable within one year without payment of compensation.

(iii) Details of the Service Contracts of the Directors of Payne having more than 12 months to run and their remuneration thereunder as follows:—

Name	Date of expiry	Annual salary and directors' fees £	Commission for 1968 £
J. E. Payne	1.12.1973	13,300	2,276
O. C. I. Spicer	1.12.1984	7,000	2,276
L. R. Crawley	1.12.1985	5,250	2,276
C. Radford	31.12.1978	4,000	1,138

P. P. Payne & Sons Limited

In addition to the Annual Salary and Directors' Fees shown, each Director is entitled to receive commission at such a rate (being not less than 1%) as shall be fixed in the case of the Chairman, by the Board of Directors, and in the case of the other Directors, by the Chairman, on the amount of the aggregate net profits of the Company before taxation. The amount of commission for 1968 is set out above.

3. MARKET QUOTATIONS

The middle market quotations as shown in the Daily Official List of The Stock Exchange, London, for the Ordinary shares of Norcros and for the $8\frac{1}{2}\%$ Cumulative Preference shares and Ordinary shares of Payne on 23rd July 1969 (the day preceding the announcement of the Offers), on the first day of dealing in each of the six months preceding the date of this Offer Letter and on 8th August 1969 (the last practicable date prior to the printing of this document), were:—

1969	Norcros Ordinary shares	Payne Preference shares	Payne Ordinary shares
3rd March	23s 0d	18s 9d xd	22s 0d
1st April	22s 6d xd	17s 6d	22s 0d xd
1st May	20s 0d	17s 6d	23s 6d
2nd June	18s 1½d	17s 6d	23s 6d
1st July	17s 6d	17s 6d	22s 0d
23rd July	16s 6d	17s 6d	21s 6d
1st August	16s 6d	17s 6d	35s 0d
8th August	17s 6d	19s 6d	34s 0d

4. FURTHER CONDITIONS OF THE OFFERS

(A) The Offer for the Ordinary shares will not be declared unconditional unless Norcros has acquired or agreed to acquire (either pursuant to the Offer or by shares acquired or agreed to be acquired before or during the Offer) over 50% of the Ordinary shares of Payne.

(B) In the case of each Offer:—

(i) Norcros will announce and simultaneously inform The Stock Exchange, London, by 9.30 a.m. on 4th September 1969, or any later date being the working day next following the expiry of any extension or revision of the Offer ('the relevant date'):—

(a) that the Offer has been declared or become unconditional, in which case Norcros will announce the total number of shares (as nearly as practicable); (i) held before the Offer was announced; (ii) accepted through the Offer; and (iii) acquired or agreed to be acquired during the Offer period by it and its associates; or

(b) that the closing date of the Offer has been extended; or

(c) that the Offer has lapsed.

(ii) If the Offer is declared unconditional but Norcros fails to comply with the requirements of paragraph (i) (a) above by 3.30 p.m. on the relevant date the unconditional declaration shall be void but Norcros shall be entitled again to declare the Offer unconditional but not before the expiry of 8 days after the relevant date.

(iii) The Offer will not be withdrawn during its currency unless:—

(*a*) the permission of the Panel on Takeovers and Mergers is received; or

(*b*) a competing Offer (if any) becomes or is declared unconditional.

(iv) If the Offer becomes or is declared unconditional or is again declared unconditional pursuant to pargraph (ii) above it will remain open for acceptance for a further minimum period of 14 days unless it becomes unconditional on 3rd September 1969, or on the expiry date of any extension and Norcros has given at least 10 days' prior notice in writing to the appropriate class of shareholders of Payne that in respect of that class of shares the Offer will not remain open for acceptance beyond 3rd September 1969, or beyond the expiry date of any extension.

(v) If sufficient acceptances are received, Norcros will apply the powers conferred by Section 209 of the Companies Act, 1948 in respect of each class of shares separately.

(vi) An acceptance of the Offer may be withdrawn by delivery of notice in writing to Hill Samuel & Co. Limited, 6 Greencoat Place, London, S.W.1, if the unconditional declaration has become void in accordance with paragraph (ii) above, but only until such time as the Offer is again declared unconditional. An acceptance of the Offer may likewise be withdrawn if by 24th September 1969, the Offer has not been declared unconditional but only until such time as the Offer is declared unconditional, being not later than 12th October 1969.

(vii) If the Offer is revised, it will be kept open for a period of at least 8 days from the date on which written notification of the revision is despatched to the shareholders of Payne. In any case, where revised consideration is offered representing on such date (on such basis as Norcros may consider appropriate) an improvement in the value of the consideration previously offered, the benefit of the improved Offer will be made available to acceptors of the Offer in its original or in its previously revised form, and for such purpose acceptance of the Offer in any such form shall constitute authority to Norcros to authorise any person to sign on behalf of any such acceptor an acceptance of the improved Offer. Such authority shall be irrevocable, if and so long as the earlier acceptance remains irrevocable, but shall be revoked automatically if the earlier acceptance becomes subject to withdrawal and is duly withdrawn.

(viii) All documents despatched by post will be sent at the risk of the person(s) entitled thereto. No acknowledgement of the receipt of documents will be sent by Hill Samuel & Co. Limited.

5. GENERAL

(i) The issue of this document has been approved by the Boards of Norcros and Payne. The Boards of each Company have considered all statements of fact and opinion contained in this document, and accept, collectively and individually, responsibility for the accuracy of all such statements of fact so far as they relate to their own Company or its subsidiaries or its Directors, and for the bona fides of any opinions expressed herein by or on behalf of their own Company or its Directors and confirm that to the best of their knowledge, information and belief, no material factors or considerations have been omitted.

(ii) Save as disclosed in this document no agreement exists between Norcros or any of its subsidiaries and any of the Directors of Payne conditional upon or in connection with the outcome of the Offers.

(iii) There is no agreement or arrangement whereby any of the shares of Payne that may be acquired by Norcros under the Offers may be transferred to any person other than a nominee of Norcros.

(iv) Hill Samuel & Co. Limited are satisfied that the necessary financial resources, being a maximum of £1,900,000, are available to Norcros to enable them to implement the Offers in full.

(v) The Directors of Norcros are satisfied that, after taking account of bank and other facilities available, Norcros has adequate working capital for its present requirements.

(vi) At 31st July 1969 the loan capital of Norcros was £2,485,210 $6\frac{3}{4}\%$ Unsecured Loan Stock, 1977/82 and £2,000,000 5% Unsecured Loan Stock 1969/71 and the loan capital and mortgages of subsidiaries amounted to £209,039. At the same date bank overdrafts and similar indebtedness of the Norcros Group amounted to £1,615,365 and outstanding hire-purchase commitments of subsidiaries amounted to £408,466. With the above exceptions neither Norcros nor any of its subsidiaries has any debentures, debenture stock, mortgages, charges or other loan capital or bank indebtedness outstanding. Except for guarantees in the ordinary course of business and of the obligations of its subsidiary, Hygena Limited, under the underlease of its factory premises and of certain obligations of a former subsidiary, for which an indemnity has been given, neither Norcros nor any of its subsidiaries has any guarantees or other contingent liabilities of material amount outstanding.

(vii) At 31st July 1969 Norcros and its subsidiaries had short-term investments including deposits with bankers amounting to £3,200,000 all of which will be realised by 20th January 1970.

(viii) The issue by Norcros of Ordinary shares under the Share Alternative does not require consent to be given by a resolution of the Ordinary shareholders of Norcros.

(ix) All expenses incidental to the preparation and circulation of the Offers and any stamp duties and transfer fees resulting from acceptances are expected to amount to £50,500 and will be paid by Norcros.

6. PROFIT FORECAST OF PAYNE

The following are copies of letters received from Prior & Palmer, Payne's auditors, and Kleinwort, Benson Limited addressed to the Directors of Payne in accordance with paragraph 15 of The City Code on Takeovers and Mergers concerning the forecast profits of Payne for the year ending 31st December 1969 contained on page 2 of this document:—

To the Directors of
P. P. Payne & Sons Limited,
Haydn Road,
Nottingham, NG5 1DL   11th August 1969

Dear Sirs,

We have reviewed the accounting bases and calculations for the profit forecast of P. P. Payne & Sons Limited (for which the directors are solely responsible) for the period of one year ending 31st December 1969 set out in your Chairman's letter of recommendation which accompanies the formal Offer document dated 13th August 1969, addressed to the Ordinary and Preference shareholders of your Company. The forecast includes the results shown by unaudited accounts for the six months ended 5th July 1969. In our opinion the forecast, so far as the accounting bases and calculations are concerned, has been properly compiled on the footing of the assumptions made by the Board contained in the said letter of recommendation and are presented on a basis consistent with the accounting practices normally adopted by the Company.

Yours faithfully,

PRIOR & PALMER.

The Directors
P. P. Payne & Sons Limited,
Haydn Road,
Nottingham, NG5 1DL   11th August 1969
Dear Sirs,

We refer to your Chairman's letter of recommendation which accompanies the formal Offer document addressed to the Ordinary and Preference shareholders of P. P. Payne & Sons Limited dated 13th August 1969.

In accordance with the requirements of paragraph 15 of The City Code on Takeovers and Mergers, we are writing in connection with the forecast of profits for the year ending 31st December 1969, contained in the said letter of recommendation.

In the course of discussions with your auditors, Messrs Prior & Palmer, there was made available to us information substantiating the assumptions on which the forecast was based, namely the interim unaudited accounts in respect of the six months to 5th July 1969, supplemented by the Company's budget statements for the year ending 31st December 1969.

We confirm that we are satisfied that the profit forecast contained in the said letter of recommendation has been made after due and careful consideration and is consistent with the budget statements referred to above.

Yours faithfully,

For KLEINWORT, BENSON LIMITED,
F. R. HISLOP,
Director.

Prior & Palmer and Kleinwort, Benson Limited have given and have not withdrawn their written consent to the publication of their respective letters in the form and context in which they appear above.

7. DOCUMENTS FOR INSPECTION

Copies of the following documents will be available for inspection at the offices of Richards, Butler & Co., Stone House, 128/140 Bishopsgate, London, E.C.2, during the usual business hours on any weekday (Saturdays and Public Holidays excepted) while the Offers remain open:

(i) The Memoranda and Articles of Association of Norcros and of Payne.
(ii) The published Accounts for the last two completed financial years of Norcros and of Payne.
(iii) The service contracts referred to in paragraph 2 (iii) above.
(iv) The above-mentioned letters and consents referred to in paragraph 6.

Exhibit 28.3 P. P. Payne & Sons Limited
Extel Cards—Norcros Ltd.
Annual Card

NI–NZ 67
ANNUAL CARD   NOR
PLEASE WITHDRAW PREVIOUS CARD
NORCROS LTD.
INDUSTRIAL GROUP. Inc. May 1956. Made Public June 1956. Reg. Office: Reading Bridge House, Reading, Berkshire. Tel.: 0734 40861. Registrars and Transfer Office: Hill, Samuel & Co. Ltd., 6 Greencoat Place, S.W.1. Tel.: 01-828 4321. Co. was formed for purpose of carrying on business as an industrial investment holding Co.
PRINCIPAL SUB. COS. (100% owned unless stated): DOW-MAC CONCRETE LTD. (Pre-cast, pre-stressed and reinforced concrete); HYGENA LTD. (Kitchen Units); LANTIGEN (ENGLAND) LTD. (Pharmaceutical products); S. MAW, SON AND SONS, LTD. (75%) (Nursery goods and pharmaceutical products); NEIL AND SPENCER LTD. (Dry-cleaning and laundry machinery for sale see over); NORPRINT LTD. (Photographic coated papers and films, labels, tickets and tags and overprinting machines); TEMPERATURE LTD. (Air conditioning and refrigeration equipment); BULK CARRIERS LTD. (Canada) (Bulk liquid road haulage). For acquisition of M. & S. Shifrin Ltd. (bedroom and dining room manufacturers), see over.
ASSOCIATED COS. Scotcros Ltd. (approx. 33% held) formed as an Industrial Holding Co. for Scottish businesses. In Sept. 1960, Co. sold 1 177 666 Ord. shares of 5s of Southcros Ltd. Co.'s Ord. holders in ratio of 1 for 9 at 5s 6d per Ord. 5s share; Beaudrey Norcros Ltd. (50%).
DIRECTORS: J. V. Sheffield (Chairman); J. J. Boex (Managing); E. C. R. Sheffield; J. P. Spencer, O.B.E.; Hon. P. M. Samuel, M.C., T.D.; D. Kirkness; F. J. Briggs; P. I. Marshall, F.C.A.; W. G. S. Tozer.
SECRETARY: V. C. Yaldren, F.C.A.
BANKERS: National Provincial Ltd.
AUDITORS: Deloitte, Plender, Griffiths & Co.

AUTHORISED	CAPITAL	ISSUED
£4 000 000 in 6½% (6% up to 31 March 1959) Cumulative		
Preference shares of £1		£2 198 327
£6 000 000 in Ordinary shares of 5s		£3 821 675

Placing price of shares to Public June 1956, 5s 3d per Ord. share. In June 1956, 100 000 Ord. shares were issued for cash. Subsequent issues of Ord. and Pref. shares have been made from time to time in connection with acquisition of further Subs. In Sept. 1956, 235 600 Ord. shares of 5s (already in issue) were offered up to Ord. holders at 17s 3d (19 for 100). At 30 June 1957. Issued capital of Co. stood at £723 000 consisting of 215 000 6% Cum. Pref. shares of £1 and 2 032 000 Ord. shares of 5s. In Aug. 1957, 50 000 Pref. and 105 371 Ord. were issued in connection with acquisition. In March 1958, 16 499 Pref. of £1 were issued as part consideration of acquisition. In April 1959, Pref. dividend was increased from 6% to 6½% and in May 1959, Capitalisation issue, 2 334 000 Ord. shares of 5s (1 for 1) (xc 27 May). In Nov. 1959, 295 000 6½% Cum. Pref. shares of £1 were issued at par. Also during 1959 a total of 446 629 Ord. shares of 5s and 423 501 Pref. shares of £1 were issued in respect of acquisitions. In May 1960 125 000 Pref. shares of £1 were issued at 20s 3d per share. In July 1960, Capitalisation issue, 5 189 500 Ord. shares of 5s (1 for 1) (xc 15 July). During 1960, 975 600 Ord. shares of 5s and 817 800 Pref. shares of £1 were issued in respect of acquisitions. In April 1961, Capitalisation issue, 3 694 367 Ord. shares of 5s (1 for 3) (xc 10 April). In April 1961, 95 527 6½% Cum. Pref. shares of £1 and 32 320 Ord. shares of 5s were issued in respect of acquisition. In Nov. 1961, 12 500 Ord. shares of 5s were issued in respect of acquisition. In Feb. 1962, 160 000 6½% Pref. shares of £1 and 450 000 Ord. shares of 5s were issued as part consideration for acquisition. For issue of Conv. Loan stock to Ord. holders in March 1962, see below. In May 1963, 3630 Ord. shares of 5s were issued against conversion of Loan stock. In May 1964, 5 150 000 Ord. shares of 5s were issued against conversion of Loan stock. In May 1965, 5355 Ord. shares of 5s were issued against conversion of Loan stock. During 1966, 152 Ord. shares of 5s were issued against conversion of Loan stock. During 1967, 126 Ord. shares of 5s were issued against conversion of Loan stock.

DIRECTORS' INTERESTS in Capital of Co. at 1 Dec. 1968: Beneficial Ord. 332 668 shares; Joint interest (including duplications) Ord. 1 987 600 shares.

VOTING: One vote per 5s capital, but Pref. vote only in certain circumstances.

DIVIDENDS: Pref. due 31 March, 30 Sept.

On a return of capital, Pref. holders will be entitled to repayment of capital together with arrears of dividend plus a premium equal to excess (if any) over nominal value of Pref. shares of average means of daily quotations during preceding six months.

	%	Per share	Announced		Paid	Holders	Ex date
1965	Int 8⅓	5d	Sept. 14	1965	Nov. 30	Oct. 18	Sept. 27
1965	Sec. Int 8⅓	5d	Feb. 25	1966	Mar. 31	Feb. 25	Feb. 28
	Fin 3⅓	2d	Feb. 25	1966	May 18	Apr. 1	Mar. 14
1966	Int 8⅓	5d	Sept. 15	1966	Nov. 30	Oct. 14	Oct. 3
1966	Fin 11⅔	7d	Feb. 21	1967	Apr. 25	Mar. 21	Mar. 13
1967	Int 8⅓	5d	Oct. 10	1967	Nov. 30	Oct. 16	Oct. 16
1967	Fin 11⅔	7d	Feb. 19	1968	Apr. 9	Mar. 8	Feb. 26
1968	Int 8⅓	5d	Aug. 26	1968	Nov. 30	Oct. 25	Oct. 14
1968	Fin 12·37	7·422d	Feb. 24	1969	Apr. 14	Mar. 7	

LOAN STOCK: 6¾% Unsecured 1977/82. Issued: £2 500 000. Outstanding: £2 485 210. Interest 31 May and 30 Nov. Redeemable 30 Nov. 1982 at par, or earlier, whole or part by drawings, on Co.'s three months' notice, on or after 1 Dec. 1977 at par. Co. may purchase stock at any time and at any price, or by private treaty at a price not exceeding 105%. Conversion rights expired 1 May 1967. Trustees: Alliance Assurance Co. Ltd. Issued March 1962 at 98% to Ord. holders (£10 stock for 60 Ord. of 5s) (xr 19 Feb.).

*5% Unsecured 1969/71. Issued: £2 000 000. Repayable £1 000 000 on 20 Dec. 1969, £500 000 on 20 Dec. 1970 and £500 000 on 20 Dec. 1971.
*Issued as consideration for acquisition of M. & S. Shifrin Ltd., see over 15 Feb. 1969.

CONSOLIDATED PROFIT AND LOSS ACCOUNT.

Year ended 30 June	Issued ordinary £	External sales £000s	Investment income £	Net profit before tax £	Corporation tax £	Income tax £	Profits tax £	Tax equalisation £	Investment allowances £	Double tax relief £	Overseas tax £	Total tax £	Min. int. £
a1957	508 000	b	—	**348 981**	—	151 799	44 017	—	—	—	—	195 816	—
1958	534 343	b	—	**680 455**	—	295 451	66 492	12 930	—	—	—	374 873	—
*30 Nov.													
c1959	1 229 500	b	2500	**1 362 470**	—	424 878	144 708	26 561	Cr. 24 386	—	—	571 761	—
1960)	2 770 775	16 670	45 982	**1 891 754**	—	756 818	231 089	20 463	Cr. 60 313	—	—	948 057	6413
1961	3 705 572	19 750	11 436	**1 886 112**	—	713 998	274 113	3436	Cr.104 791	Cr. 3473	58 937	942 220	45 353
1962	3 818 072	24 340	30 012	**1 944 839**	—	734 657	277 435	1792	Cr. 83 697	Cr. 6552	94 417	1 018 052	35 523
1963	3 818 980	25 860	32 832	**1 990 316**	—	727 851	307 384	48 578	Cr.151 753	Cr. 8090	102 303	1 026 273	31 781
1964	3 820 267	23 000	e85 834	**2 066 063**	—	761 725	295 656	900	Cr.135 471	Cr. 9407	104 655	1 018 058	48 797
1965	3 821 606	22 301	e167 270	**1 932 671**	r 731 410	Cr.18 121	—	Cr.20 000	Cr. 63 452	Cr.11 860	130 167	748 144	86 900
d1966	3 821 644	26 790	39 492	**1 943 654**	r 799 367	53 708	—	Cr. 9300	Cr. 10 062	—	128 020	961 733	16 426
1967	3 821 675	28 205	52 324	**1 878 646**	s 665 036	—	—	23 000	—	Cr. 411	113 227	800 852	28 487
1968	3 821 675	27 965	36 484	**2 361 546**	w864 474	—	—	Cr.28 500	—	—	117 866	953 840	28 416

Year ended	Profit attrib. to parent co.	$6\frac{1}{2}$%(6) pref. div.	Profit after preference dividend	% On ordinary, less tax Earned	Paid	Retained profit for year	Charges Depre- ciation	Loan stk. int.	Loan cap. int.	Bank interest	Plant &c. hire	Dirs.' emlts.	†Excpl. items. excld.
30 June	£	£	£			£	£	£	£	£	£	£	£
a1957	**153 165**	g 1192	151 973	h49·9	Int $12\frac{1}{2}$ Sec. Int $12\frac{1}{2}$	83 872	25 472	12 468		b	b	6047	—
1958	**305 582**	9427	296 155	96·4	Int $17\frac{1}{2}$ Fin $7\frac{1}{2}$	219 343	90 420	12 980		b	b	11 406	—
*30 Nov.													
c1959	**790 709**	23 196	767 513	i101·9	Spec. Div. 15 Int 20 Cap. 100 Sec. Int 10 Fin 20	424 026	255 131	25 325		—	b	25 735	—
1960	**937 284**	42 301	894 983	j 52·7	Cap. 100 Int 11 Fin 15 Cap. $33\frac{1}{3}$	461 892	397 697	24 288		—	b	34 489	—
1961	**898 539**	79 249	819 290	k35·0	Int n $8\frac{1}{3}$ Fin k $11\frac{2}{3}$	357 478	803 276	22 418		61 109	b	38 017	—
1962	**891 264**	87 521	803 743	34·4	Int $8\frac{1}{3}$ Fin $11\frac{2}{3}$	336 029	847 369	108 000	20 502	76 877	b	35 774	—
1963	**932 262**	87 521	844 741	36·1	Int $8\frac{1}{3}$ Fin $11\frac{2}{3}$	376 918	936 711	168 527	19 249	21 637	b	p44 182	—
1964	**999 208**	87 521	911 687	40·3	Int $8\frac{1}{3}$ Fin $11\frac{2}{3}$	454 846	959 173	168 178	16 757	48 135	b	28 480	—
1964				q24·0									
1965	**1 097 627**	85 735	1 011 892	25·0	Int $8\frac{1}{3}$ Sec. Int $8\frac{1}{3}$ Fin $3\frac{1}{3}$	562 854	703 843	167 777	14 887	43 572	b	31 927	—
d1966	**965 495**	u142 891	822 604	21·5	Int $8\frac{1}{3}$ Fin $11\frac{2}{3}$	u58 276	802 031	167 764	13 017	68 875	193 310	t109 689	—
1967	**1 049 307**	142 891	906 416	23·7	Int $8\frac{1}{3}$ Fin $11\frac{2}{3}$	142 081	816 539	176 719		v130 094	156 551	55 658	—
1968	**1 379 290**	142 891	1 236 399	32·4	Int $8\frac{1}{3}$ Fin 12·37	445 312	756 524	175 842		v169 302	154 698	86 962	—

AVERAGE NUMBER OF UK EMPLOYEES: 1965, 5726; 1966, 6032; 1967, 6172; 1968, 5661 (Remuneration, £6 304 500).

*Approx. †Exceptional items excluded from profit shown in accounts. (a) Parent Co. for period from 29 May 1956, and Sub. Cos. from date of acquisition. (b) Not disclosed. (c) 17 months. (d) Including profits of Ward, Brooke & Co. Ltd. from 25 March 1966 and losses of Profile Publication Ltd. from 10 Dec. 1965. (e) Including £48 980 dividend from Subsidiary sold during year in 1964 and £127 660 in 1965. (g) On £65 000 Pref. capital for period. (h) For comparison, earnings calculated on £508 000 capital after allowing for one year's dividend on £215 000 Pref. capital. (i) On £1 229 500 capital, equivalent to 71·9% p.a. (j) On £2 770 775 capital. (k) On £3 818 072 capital. (n) On £3 703 447 capital. (p) Including £10 000 paid on termination of employment of a Director. (q) Estimated earnings after allowing for Corporation Tax at 40%. (r) At 40%. (s) At 40% to 31 March 1967 and at $42\frac{1}{2}$% thereafter. (t) Including £60 000 compensation, less Corporation tax, to former Directors of a Sub. on termination of service agreements. (u) Dividends deducted gross though partly net in accounts (Income tax deducted from dividends and retained £37 471. (v) Interest on bank loans, overdrafts and loans wholly repayable within 5 years. (w) at $42\frac{1}{2}$%.

PRIORITY PERCENTAGES (CONSOLIDATED):

	$6\frac{3}{4}$% Loan stock (net)	$6\frac{1}{2}$% Pref.	Ordinary	Retained profit	Total earnings
†1966	£100 658	£142 891	£764 328	£58 276	£1 066 153
1967	97 855	142 891	764 335	142 081	1 147 162
1968	96 457	142 891	791 087	445 312	1 475 747
	%	%	%	%	—
	0–$6\frac{1}{2}$	$6\frac{1}{2}$–$16\frac{1}{4}$	$16\frac{1}{4}$–$69\frac{3}{4}$	$69\frac{3}{4}$–100	—

†Dividends shown gross though partly net in accounts.

ANALYSIS OF SALES AND PROFITS.

		Construction and engineering £ 000s	Consumer products £ 000s	Printing £ 000s	Overseas and other interests £ 000s	*Head office £ 000s	Total £ 000s	UK £ 000s	Exports from UK £ 000s	Overseas £ 000s	Total £ 000s
1966	Sales	9831	5403	4978	6578		26 790	21 862	2706	2222	26 790
	Profits	541	296	513	399	154	1903				
1967	Sales	10 274	6099	5307	6525		28 205	22 944	2648	2613	28 205
	Profits	574	401	638	136	130	1879				
1968	Sales	9795	7372	5822	4976		27 965	21 981	3196	2788	27 965
	Profits	621	466	832	410	33	2362				

*Interest less expenses.

CONSOLIDATED HALF YEARLY FIGURES (UNAUDITED). (To end of May approx.).

	Sales UK £ 000s	Sales Exports £ 000s	Sales Overseas £ 000s	Sales Total £ 000s	*Trading profit £ 000s	Depreciation £ 000s	H/O expenses £ 000s	Interest £ 000s	Profit bef. tax £ 000s	Tax £ 000s	Min. int. £ 000s	Attrib. to group £ 000s	Earned for ord. £ 000s	P/S.
1966	a	a	a	12 205	b1334	353	d43		838	366	8	464	a	a
1967	11 202	1243	985	13 430	1476	416	141	138	781	327	7	447	376	5·9d
†1968	11 014	1561	1317	13 892	1745	386	193	168	998	407	8	583	512	8·0d

*Includes Investment Income. †Excludes Jensen Motors Ltd., sold 22 Aug. 1968. (a) Not disclosed. (b) Excludes Investment Income. (c) After deducting Investment Income.

LONDON PRICES OF 5s ORDINARY SHARES.

Calendar Year	†1960	†1961	1962	1963	1964	1965	1966	1967	1968	*1969
Highest	49s 4d	28s 10d	17s 9d	17s 4d	15s 10d	14s 10d	13s 3d	14s 1d	25s 10d	27s 7d
Lowest	20s 0d	14s 9d	11s 6d	13s 3d	12s 10d	11s 0d	7s 4d	8s 7d	11s 0d	23s 7d

*To 17 Feb. †Adjusted to give effect to Capitalisation issues: 1960, Prices prior to Capitalisation to 6 July, 71s 40s;— Quotation 14 July, 83s 78s; 1961, 5 April, 38s 6d, 31s 9d;—Quotation 7 April, 33s 28s.

P. P. Payne & Sons Limited

GROSS YIELD INDICATOR 20·7% Dividend, 32·4% Earnings. £3 821 675 Capital.

PRICE		18s 0d	19s 0d	20s 0d	21s 0d	22s 0d	23s 0d	24s 0d	25s 0d	26s 0d
DIVIDEND YIELD	%	5·75	5·45	5·17	4·93	4·70	4·50	4·31	4·14	3·98
EARNINGS YIELD	%	9·00	8·53	8·10	7·71	7·36	7·04	6·75	6·48	6·23
P/E RATIO		11·11	11·73	12·35	12·96	13·58	14·20	14·81	15·43	16·05

CONSOLIDATED BALANCE SHEETS.

	3 December 1967 £	1 December 1968 £
CAPITAL	6 020 002	6 020 002
CAPITAL RESERVES		
Share Premium	275 749	275 749
Loan Capital Redemption	225 800	123 300
General	898 038	965 690
REVENUE RESERVES		
General	895 000	810 000
Profit & Loss Account	2 091 992	2 660 227
6¾% CONVERTIBLE LOAN STOCK	2 485 210	2 485 210
LOAN CAPITAL OF SUBS.	174 200	136 700
TAX EQUALISATION	244 500	374 442
MINORITY INTEREST	237 262	243 991
DUE UNDER HP CONTRACTS	121 827	133 132
CORPORATION TAX	714 074	808 443
	£14 383 654	£15 036 886

	3 December 1967 £	1 December 1968 £
CURRENT ASSETS		
Stocks & Work	4 378 641	4 210 125
Debtors, &c	5 733 295	7 230 346
Cash	124 311	317 597
	10 236 247	11 758 068
CURRENT LIABILITIES	6 198 900	*6 867 468
NET CURRENT ASSETS	4 037 347	4 890 600
FIXED ASSETS		
Land & Buildings		
Freehold	2 177 154	†2 813 936
Leasehold	970 673	‡1 044 909
Plant, &c	2 275 973	§1 896 252
Vehicles	1 087 197	¶1 230 140
Patents, Rights, &c.	17 056	—
GOODWILL	3 414 254	2 805 444
INVESTMENTS	404 000	⊕355 605
	£14 383 654	£15 036 886

*Due under HP Contracts £163 429 (1967, £126 497); Creditors £4 974 570 (£4 343 022); Overdraft £1 256 855 (£1 283 519); Final Ord. Dividend £472 614 (£445 862). †At Directors' valuation 1 Dec. 1968; after £63 084 depreciation. ‡At Directors' valuation 1 Dec. 1968; after £117 553 depreciation. §At cost; after £2 651 520 depreciation.¶At cost; after £2 072 091 depreciation.⊕Quoted £262 917 (market value £359 205); Unquoted £92 688 (Directors' valuation £92 688).
Note (1968): Investments and Building Grants totalling £225 800 have been deducted from cost of relative assets.
NET ASSET VALUE (BOOK VALUE). Excluding intangibles, at B/s. date per 5s Ordinary share: 1968, 7s 8d.

ACQUISITION OF M. & S. SHIFRIN LTD. AND SALE OF SUB. Co. ('Norcros') has acquired M. & S. Shifrin Ltd. ('Shifrin'). A conditional sale of agreement has been entered into for sale to Gomaco Equipment Sales Ltd. ('Gomaco') of Neil and Spencer Ltd. ('Neil and Spencer'). For year to 30 June 1969, vendors of Shifrin expect that profits will, in absence of unforeseen circumstances, amount to £300 000 before tax. Consideration payable for Shifrin is £2 000 000 satisfied by issue of £2 000 000 5% Unsecured Loan Stock. Loan stock will not be quoted on any Stock Exchange.

Sale of Neil and Spencer to Gomaco is in accordance with policy of Board to concentrate Group's interest in a selected range of activities. Proceeds of sale which will amount to £3 000 000 will be utilised in growth of existing Group and for further expansion by suitable acquisitions. Completition of sale is expected to take place in mid-March. In addition to all share capital. Norcros interest in Neil and Spencer includes loans amounting to £1 440 000. Consideration for sale of shares amounts to £1 560 000 payable in cash and Gomaco has undertaken to secure repayment of loans, making total cash receivable £3 000 000 on completion. Book value of net tangible assets attributable to share capital, as shown by the latest audited accounts dated 1 Dec. 1968, amounted to £419 217. Norcros will therefore make a profit of £1 140 783 which will be subject to capital gains tax estimated not to exceed £170 000.

EARNINGS. Effect on earnings of Norcros Group of purchase of Shifrin and disposal of Neil and Spencer can be estimated as follows, assuming (a) that earnings of Shifrin will amount to £300 000 p.a. and (b) that other earnings of Group will remain at level achieved in year ended 1 Dec. 1968:— Earnings before tax will be increased by £163 250 and after tax at $42\frac{1}{2}\%$ earnings for Ord. shareholders will be increased by £93 625 equivalent to 1·5d per share.

Mr J. P. Spencer, Chairman and Managing Director and founder of Neil and Spencer is also a Director of Norcros. Following completion Mr Spencer will resign from Board of Norcros without compensation.

24 March 1969.

REPORT for year ended 1 Dec. 1968. For figures, see tables. Carry forward £2 660 227 (£2 091 992).

FINANCE ACT, 1965. Co. is not a 'close Co.'.

CHAIRMAN'S STATEMENT. During 1968 Board had to take some fundamental decisions with regard to disposal of Cos. deemed no longer relevant to Group's new concept. First of these was Jensen Motors Ltd., which was sold in Aug. of last year. They also disposed of Bramigk & Co. Ltd. All operating Cos. have increased their profitability during year, which has resulted in highest pre-tax profit in Co.'s history.

LATER INFORMATION WILL BE PUBLISHED ON NEWS CARD.

NEWS CARD

NORCROS LTD.

NEWS CARD   UP-DATED TO 4–9–69
PLEASE WITHDRAW PREVIOUS NEWS CARD

GROSS YIELD INDICATOR based on 20·7% Dividend. 32·4% (1·62s per share) Earnings. £3 821 675 Capital.

PRICE	13s 0d	14s 0d	15s 0d	16s 0d	17s 0d	18s 0d	19s 0d
DIVIDEND YIELD %	7·96	7·39	6·90	6·47	6·09	5·75	5·45
EARNINGS YIELD %	12·46	11·57	10·80	10·13	9·53	9·00	8·53
P/E RATIO	8·02	8·64	9·26	9·88	10·49	11·11	11·73

SHARE PRICES. 5s ORD. (LONDON): 1969, Highest 27s 7d, Lowest 14s 7d. To 18 Aug.

ORD. DIVIDEND PAYMENT DETAILS. Year end 30 Nov. (approx.). Last accounts published 24 Mar. 1969.

	%	Per share	Announced	Paid	Holders	Ex date
1966	Int 8⅓	5d	Sept. 15 1966	Nov. 30	Oct. 14	Oct. 3
1966	Fin 11⅔	7d	Feb. 21 1967	Apr. 25	Mar. 21	Mar. 13
1967	Int 8⅓	5d	Oct. 10 1967	Nov. 30	Oct. 16	Oct. 16
1967	Fin 11⅔	7d	Feb. 19 1968	Apr. 9	Mar. 8	Feb. 26
1968	Int 8⅓	5d	Aug. 26 1968	Nov. 30	Oct. 25	Oct. 14
1968	Fin 12·37	7·422d	Feb. 24 1969	Apr. 14	Mar. 7	Mar. 10
1969	Int 8⅓	5d	Aug. 14 1969	Nov. 29	Oct. 24	

CONSOLIDATED HALF YEARLY FIGURES (UNAUDITED). (To end of May approx.).

	Sales				*Trading	Depre-
	UK	Exports	Overseas	Total	profit	ciation
	£ 000s	£ 000s	£ 000s	£ 000s	£ 000s	£ 000s
1966	a	a	a	12 205	b1334	353
1967	11 202	1243	985	13 430	1476	416
†1968	11 014	1561	1317	13 892	1745	386
1969	10 169	806	1393	12 368	1833	379

	H/O		Profit		Min.	Attrib.	Earned	
	expenses	Interest	bef. tax	Tax	int.	to group	for ord.	
	£ 000s	£ 000s	£ 000s	£ 000s	£ 000s	£ 000s	£ 000s	P/S.
1966	d43		838	366	8	464	a	a
1967	141	138	781	327	7	447	376	5·9d
1968	193	168	998	407	8	583	512	8·0d
1969	169	199	1086	491		595	524	8·2d

*Includes Investment Income. †Excludes Jensen Motors Ltd., sold 22-1968.
(a) Not disclosed. (b) Excludes Investment Income. (c) After deducting Investment Income.

6 June 1969
ACQUISITION. Co. through its newly formed Australian Sub., Sorcron Pty. Ltd. has acquired 70% control of Raymond Holdings of Sydney for a consideration of \$A525 000 (£245 000) in cash.

Estimated annual profits of Raymond Holdings are \$A148 000 (£69 000) before tax and \$A85 000 (£39 500) after tax. Through its Sub. Label House, Raymond Holdings is leading Co. in Australia and New Zealand in field of speciality label and ticket printing. It has factories in Sydney, Melbourne, Wellington, Auckland and Singapore.